The Last Machine

Early Cinema and the Birth of the Modern World

Ian Christie

Terry Gilliam as Méliès' man in the moon

Contents

The Emperor's Old Clothes

History's a funny business. Recently, someone was doing research on my background and they stumbled on an intriguing fact I never knew: my grandfather had run a cinema in Des Moines, Iowa. Amazingly my mother had never told me this—probably didn't want to encourage another black sheep in the family.

I grew up thinking that the great film-makers created their films with an utter clarity and sureness of vision, knowing every frame of the finished film before the cameras began to roll. Of course it isn't like that. More often than not, the good things are the result of a much messier, and less easy to write about, process.

When I was a kid I used to do magic shows, which is why I've always admired Georges Méliès, the father of all film magicians. He didn't just invent almost all the special effects still used today, he put whole worlds of magic and nonsense on the screen. Anyone who makes the kind of films I do can't help but respect and admire Méliès.

I started my working life as a cartoonist and that's what some of the first film-makers were before this strange new profession opened up. They already knew how to tell stories with pictures on the page. When they discovered how to do this on film the result was what we call animation. I became an animator in the same fashion—stumbling about in the dark trying to breathe life into my static drawings.

The most important lesson I learned was that anything's possible, which is what still inspires me. When you look at the very first films, you can actually see people discovering a brand-new language—revelling in the power of a close-up, a cut or a dissolve.

Film-makers have been the storytellers of this century and even with all the new electronic media, I think storytelling will remain crucial. I'm a storyteller who happens to be adept in this medium. I grew up with it and I love the scale of it. But it's really just our own version of sitting outside in the night around a flickering campfire, with voices coming out of the darkness telling tales that mesmerise, titillate, or scare the hell out of you.

There was a documentary I once saw about an Amazonian shaman who took his assistant to the cinema for the first time. The young man came out terrified. Nothing made sense. One moment a person would be standing far away ... the next moment his face filled the screen. Utter confusion. Time and space were ripped apart. We take this for granted, we understand the vocabulary and grammar of film, and our kids seem to be born with it, but to an innocent from the jungle this meant only one thing—the dream of death.

That sorcerer's apprentice had managed to see through our latest, and most powerful, emperor's new clothes. The movies are a primal thing as much as a modern machine. They're about our most basic experiences, fears and pleasures. And *The Last Machine* takes us back to the beginning of that dream.

Terry Gilliam

Acknowledgments

This book and the television series it accompanies were prompted by the centenary of cinema due to be celebrated throughout Europe in 1995–96. It follows the thematic structure of the series, with two additional framing chapters. Both the book and television programmes aim to convey to a wider audience than specialists some of the excitement that has accompanied the study of early cinema since the 1970s. They draw freely on the growing body of research which has already turned what until recently was known as 'archaeology' into the liveliest field of cinema studies today.

Many have contributed directly and indirectly to making the book and the series possible. I owe a particular debt to Colin MacCabe who, as Head of Research at the British Film Institute, originally commissioned the project and saw it through the first stage of definition. I am also grateful to Wilf Stevenson for enabling me to concentrate on it as part of the Institute's contribution to the centenary. Other BFI colleagues helped in various ways: Clyde Jeavons, Anne Fleming and Christine Kirby of the National Film and Television Archive were supportive, while Luke McKernan generously shared his expertise in early cinema. Heather Stewart, Ed Buscombe, Erich Sargeant, Richard Paterson, Stephen Herbert and Charles Glyn also helped beyond the call of duty.

The television series was produced through Illuminations Television and John Wyver has been a valued, sympathetic partner throughout. As director, Richard Curson Smith worked tirelessly to make it accessible and imaginative; both the series and the book owe a great deal to his creative involvement. Many others helped make the series a truly collaborative project, in particular Ian Astridge, Emma Bailey, Gordon Baskerville, Jeff Baynes, Penny Beard, Charlotte Butler, Paul Cheetham, Denise Douieb, Keith Griffiths, John Lunn, Ben McPherson, Charles Staffell, Matthew Stonehouse, Alan Taylor and Robert Ziegler.

Many archives provided invaluable resources and generous advice. Particular thanks are due to: Michelle Aubert and the staff of the CNC Service des Archives at Bois d'Arcy, France; Hoos Blotkamp and the staff of the Nederlands Film Museum; David Francis and the staff of the Library of Congress Motion Picture Division in Washington DC; Mary Lea Bandy and the staff of the Museum of Modern Art Film Department in New York; and Jan-Christopher Horak and the staff of the Film Department at George Eastman House in Rochester, New York. Equal thanks are due to Madeleine Malthête-Méliès for advice and access to her grandfather's films, to Maud Linder for similar assistance with the films of her father, and to Val Williamson for permission to use the films of Cecil Hepworth.

This project has drawn heavily on the work of many scholars. My main debts are to Noël Burch, who has done so much to open up the study of early cinema, to Richard Abel, John Barnes, Stephen Bottomore, Kevin Brownlow, Michael Chanan, John Fell, Tom Gunning, Paul Hammond, Miriam Hansen, Charles Musser, David Robinson, Barry Salt, Paul Spehr,

Emmanuelle Toulet, Linda Williams and to many fellow-members of Domitor, the international society for the study of early cinema. Special thanks are due to Yuri Tsivian and to Roland Cosandey, old friends and valued advisers on *The Last Machine*. I hope they will feel their advice has borne fruit. And I hope also that the Pordenone Silent Film Festival, the Giornate del Cinema Muto, through which I have gained much of my first-hand contact with early cinema and its scholars, will receive the support it deserves and continue its unique, inspiring work.

At the BBC, *The Last Machine* has had the benefit of consistent enthusiasm from Michael Jackson and Chris Lent, and from Steve Pollock; and at VPRO Television in Holland Harry Hosman and the late Roelof Kiers have been supportive co-production partners. With typical generosity, Terry Gilliam allowed his love of early cinema to draw him into the project at a busy time in his own schedule. His involvement has been an encouragement to us all— and a lot of fun.

Acknowledgment is due to George Sassoon and Faber and Faber for permission to quote Siegfried Sassoon's poem *Picture-Show*; and to the National Gallery of Victoria, Australia, for permission to reproduce *The Rescue* by Sir John Millais, from the Felton Bequest; and to the estate of Ernest Shepard for *The Wind in the Willows* illustration. Stills of Méliès' films and posters are by courtesy of Madeleine Malthête-Méliès and of Max Linder by courtesy of Maud Linder. The majority of illustrations come from the collections of BFI Stills, Posters and Designs and from the Science Museum. Other stills and images are from the collections of Theodore X. Barber, Q. David Bowers, Kevin Brownlow, Brian Coe, Donald Crafton, Charles Musser, Serge Nazarieff, Barry Salt, Emmanuelle Toulet and Yuri Tsivian, and from the archives of Gaumont and Pathé. The front cover photograph of Terry Gilliam is by Sarah Ainslie and the Contents picture is mine.

I am grateful for advice, feedback and references to Edward, Isabel, Laura and Beatrice Christie, Robert Christie, Susie and Carl Heap, Elizabeth Lebas, Muriel Nightingale, and Deac Rossell. Christine Gordon has helped invaluably with research and liaison, and John Pym has been a sympathetic editor. But my main debt, as ever, is to Patsy Nightingale, who has miraculously enabled *The Last Machine* and our family life to co-exist.

Ian Christie
September 1994

In memory of my Mother,
who loved movies;
and in gratitude to my Father,
even though he's still not sure they're a good idea

A prediction of the audiovisual telephone from *Punch* in 1879

Hollis Frampton was a visionary film-maker whose understanding of what film could be was as radical as that of his friend Carl André (of bricks fame) in sculpture. He had been a youthful protégé of Ezra Pound and a photographer, especially of the New York art world of the sixties. His occasional writings about photography and film have a rare wit and authority. Swift, Pater and Pound seemed to him better guides than modern historians who lacked a sense of irony and awe. So he used allegories and outrageous jokes to help us see what a strange affair photography and later film were.

Were? Frampton had no doubt that both still photography and cinema already belonged to a previous age, the Age of Machines. Typically, he proposed radar as the avatar of the new age, rather than the more usual video. The aim was to provoke reflection, rather than follow received opinion. Of course we still live in a world of machines, but we can see—even more clearly than Frampton could a quarter of a century ago—that the initiative has passed to systems which are fundamentally different from machines.

What survives from an age, Frampton claimed, is the distinctive art form it invents for itself. That art will be the result of one era's physical needs becoming a means of 'psychic survival' in the next: it is what comforts, nourishes and inspires amid change and uncertainty. But if 'no activity can become an art until its proper epoch has ended', then the obsolescence of machines was precisely a precondition for cinema to become art. At least some cinema, for Frampton is keen to remind us that 'the likes of *Battleship Potemkin* make up a numbingly small fraction' of cinema as a whole, which includes 'instructional films, sing-alongs' and medical cinematography.

Frampton's ideas, however rhetorical they may sound to sober historians, seem to offer a better guide to understanding that late-Victorian world which stumbled upon cinema than approaches which are either resolutely archaeological or wishfully modern. At the centenary of moving pictures, we need somehow to find an imaginative way of linking what the pioneers and their contemporaries *thought* was happening with what mysteriously emerged in less than a decade as cinema.

This book draws freely upon nearly two decades of intensive study of 'early cinema' which has called into question much of what was widely accepted as history for fifty years. For those who never knew the old shibboleths, much of this corrective industry will seem merely academic. So too may the heroic efforts of scholars to find better ways of classifying and describing what actually happens in early films. Discussions of 'framing', 'point of view' and 'match-cutting' can seem myopic when confronted with the Rabelaisian vulgarity and ambition of early cinema—an all but lost continent of invention and discovery.

But the scholarship has been, and continues to be, vital. For it has forced attention away from a select number of the random collection of early films that has survived—the 'classics'—and encouraged many to look at the corpus as a whole. No longer just the well-loved *Rescued by Rover* (Hepworth, 1905), but 'chase' and 'rescue' films by the dozen, with all their national differences and international borrowings. And not only the 'first' Lumière programmes of 1895 and 1896, but almost their entire catalogue of 2,000 'views' is now accessible through the French national archive.

It is also a new generation of scholars who have insisted on looking not only at the screen, but behind and in front of it. For the films that we see in modern copies, often on video or on editing machines, can only be a part of the story of early cinema—perhaps not even the most important part. No one went to see a *particular* film until around 1907 at the very earliest. They went to the biograph, the cinematograph, the moving pictures, the nickelodeon: it was a *place* and an *experience* long before identifiable works and their makers emerged to claim their niche in history.

So we need to find out about the buildings and how people learned to behave in them. Also to trace the intermediaries—the distributors, exhibitors, publicists, commentators—who shaped this typical art of the late Machine Age. And of course we need to remember always what *else* moving picture suppliers and consumers saw and thought and took for granted, since we can scarcely imagine that film loomed large in many lives for some time. What space or need was there in the common culture of 1900 that proved so ready to be filled by his strange new activity?

Let us begin on the cusp of the century. I am looking at a copy of the *Daily Mail* dated 31 December 1900. It is a special edition 'to Commemorate the Dawn of the Twentieth Century', originally printed in gold ink. Among all its articles looking back at the old century and forward to the new, I search for a mention of moving pictures as the invention that will surely blossom in the coming century. Surprisingly, there is none. And like Conan Doyle's 'dog that did nothing', that seems curious.

What does it mean? Five years had passed since the Lumières' first public demonstration of their Cinématographe. Within months a dozen other inventors had entered the field with variations on the same basic idea. Some thousands of people in many countries were already watching films regularly. But still no mention in a stocktaking at the turn of the century.

Does it mean that we have all been misled by hindsight, imagining the huge social impact of cinemagoing could already be foreseen? In fact this newspaper is full of predictions—about submarines, powered flight, wireless telephony, the growth of cities (Birkenhead and Cardiff are expected to outstrip London!) and women's fashion (good riddance to the crinoline, but a fervent wish that that 'bifurcated garments' should be confined to the gymnasium). So was cinema simply less novel and noteworthy than we imagine? Or was it still so scattered and intermittent in its appearances that it did not yet seem like any single *thing*?

Another possibility is that this revealed a peculiarly British lack of response to novelty; or that such a low-class entertainment seemed unworthy of note by the great and the good of the time. Perhaps in other countries we will find that excited and far-sighted response which seems absent here?

There is some truth in all of these speculations, although it would be misleading to favour any one. Probably the most important conclusion to draw from a lack of early public comment is that few yet knew just what the new medium was. Was it a new way of doing familiar things, or something new for which no clear purpose yet existed?

Of course, for some time it was both—part of the typical variety and fun-fair style of entertainment, and also a novelty in its own right. But first it was magic, in an age that already used the term routinely for its common entertainment medium, the Magic Lantern. One of the century's favourite works of popular literature, *The Rubáiyát of Omar Khayyám*, had

A Victorian lantern show

already linked it with the traditional Eastern shadow theatre and offered this as a metaphor for human existence:

For in and out, above, about, below,
'Tis nothing but a magic shadow-show,
Played in a box whose candle is the sun,
Round which we phantom figures come and go.

The magic was now in the movement. We forget too easily that the usual form of the very earliest shows of both Edison's Kinetoscope and the Lumière projector was to begin with a still image which then *started to move*. Nothing impressed the first spectators as much as this demonstration, which fully justified the florid claim in 1896 of Edison's Scottish assistant, William Dickson, to have produced 'the crown and flower of nineteenth century magic'.

This was an effect which soon became impossible to reproduce, when brighter and hotter lamps meant that film stopped in the projector was likely to catch fire. Similarly, the two other most striking effects of early moving pictures—being able to vary their speed and reverse it—were also lost to mainstream cinema when sound required speeds to be stabilised and synchronised. Only amateur and 'experimental' cinema preserved these spectacular freedoms of the early period—until video allowed a wider return to the childhood of the moving image.

Once the initial fascination of this new ability to capture movement had been assimilated, it was astonishing how quickly film penetrated the culture at large. Kings and queens and presidents were all 'taken' (the language of portrait photography was the only one available) within a few years, and duly admired the results at special screenings. Pope Leo XIII appeared before Dickson's Mutoscope camera in 1898 and gave a blessing, which raised the intriguing theological question as to whether all who saw the resulting peepshow were automatically blessed—a problem about the film image's reality status which has continued to bedevil films on religious subjects.

Another thought-provoking 'first' was a 1901 Biograph film of the Chinese dignitary Li Hung Chang, seen in a courtyard of the Beijing Palace of Roses being shown a portable 'Parlor Mutoscope'. What Li is watching, we understand, is a moving picture of himself, taken three years earlier when he visited the United States. The idea of seeing this veteran of the Taiping Rebellion of some forty years earlier viewing his own 'exotic' image must surely have given its original viewers some sense of history made visible—as well as being a shrewd celebrity endorsement for the Mutoscope.

The Pope and Li Hung Chang were in good company. Statesmen, writers, artists, actors and scientists were all being filmed by the early years of the century, as a novel kind of 'life mask' for posterity. But these were only the most obvious, public uses to which the new machine was put. Behind them lay a vast network of experiments, applications and speculations—much larger than conventional cinema history has ever acknowledged. What has prevented this acknowledgment is, as Frampton observed, the dominance of the 'feature' film, a form which emerged around 1912–13 and rapidly became the 'industry standard' and also, in a kind of mirror image, the critical standard. By the time cinema history started to be written in the twenties, earlier and shorter films of most kinds already seemed marginal to the main thrust of the fiction feature film.

Each of the chapters that follow traces one theme as it reached the screen in the period up to 1913, trying to identify what was already present in the existing culture and then how cinema affected it. The themes are: travel, the city, the human body, the visible world, and the supernatural. Naturally these do not pretend to be comprehensive, and there are many other possible candidates. Equally interesting would be, for instance: art, sport, zoology, colonialism, the past, and the future. Indeed a telling exercise is to make a list of practices and subjects current at the turn of the century and see if any of these can *not* be credibly linked with the early growth of cinema.

The kinds of linkage to be found are not only through dramatic portrayal or documentary record, as in films 'about' travel, the city, the body, etc. Some are instances of trying to use film techniques within other practices. For instance, Yuri Tsivian relates that the directors of the Moscow Art Theatre considered the 1900-style cinematograph show, with its staccato rhythm of unrelated items, as a model for the production of Pushkin's 'unstageable' *Boris Godunov*. How many other works and projects of the 1900s may have been influenced in similar ways, without leaving any evidence of the fact? One thinks of Debussy's *Preludes*, Hardy's *The Dynasts*, and certainly much French vanguard painting of the Fauve and Cubist period. That there is so little proof of influence says more about the casualness of early cinemagoing and the preconceptions of biographers than about cinema's pervasive impact.

For it undoubtedly was pervasive. Moving pictures were being woven into the very fabric of daily life—with shops offering film shows to their customers, restaurants showing films and devising cinema-related meals and dishes, popular music taking up screen themes, fiction in magazines and novels using film stories, and 'picture palaces' sprouting in every town. Even James Joyce tried his luck as a Dublin cinema proprietor in 1909.

Moving pictures appeared amid other entertainments, but soon carved out their own space. The history of cinema buildings has already attracted some attention, but less has been paid to cinema behaviour and experience. What did it feel like? How did early audiences find time for film-going? Did they stop doing other things, or was this a new item on the early-twentieth-century agenda?

The ordinary film-goers—as distinct from the artists in search of a new experience and the wealthy slumming—were for the most part discovering a new experience. The working week had gradually become shorter during the last quarter of the nineteenth century, while the great cities of the Old and New World had swelled with immigrants from far and near. There was a potential demand for cheap entertainment which could not be satisfied by existing forms of theatre or by saloons and dance-halls. The 'match' between the movies and their early audience was vividly described by an early American sociologist in 1907:

I shall not soon forget a Saturday evening when I stood among the crowd of pleasure-seekers on Fifth Avenue [in Pittsburgh], and watched the men and women packed thick at the entrance of every picture-show ... They were determined to be amused, and this was one of the things labeled 'Amusement'. They were hot and tired and irritable, but willing to wait until long after our enthusiasm was dampened.

Although written by a middle-class outsider, this account has the virtue of bringing alive what is often discussed in merely aggregate terms. Much of the other evidence available is sketchy, or negative. There were reports from Britain around this time of a reduction in the crime rate after cinemas opened in some districts; and also of children playing truant from school on a large scale.

Cinemagoing had not started as a proletarian pastime. The first Lumière posters show a distinctly middle-class range of types queuing to see the cinematograph, which seems to be an accurate portrayal of its appeal. But by the early 1900s, it had acquired a vulgar, proletarian—and in North America an immigrant—image. Against this, we can reason that there were undoubtedly different audiences for cinemas in different districts. But there is a danger of forgetting the most important fact: it was largely a *new* audience, unused to *being* an audience, and certainly to the novel experience of sitting in the dark before an automated 'magic shadow-show'.

How can we grasp what this experience meant? The Russian film director Andrei Tarkovsky suggested that what cinema audiences really crave is time: 'time lost or spent or not yet had'. Could it be that early audiences discovered moving pictures gave them an expanded and concentrated experience of time—*more* time for their modest outlay? For many, the experience also seems to have been a new kind of fantasy. Like Hans Christian Andersen's Little Match Girl, they were fascinated by the luminous

The Land Beyond the Sunset (Dawley, 1912)

images that flared up out of darkness and briefly transported their viewers to another world.

Some inkling of these fantasies can be got from fiction of the period and from the films themselves. A British story from 1904 entitled 'The Cinematograph Train' treats the most famous early film experience, that of a train entering a station, in a surprising way. Young Bobbie is taken to the Small Hall in Langham Place for his first experience of the cinematograph and, after a fire engine, a troopship and the King, he sees a train rushing towards a country station platform, where it stops 'just in time':

Bobbie never knew how it was, but suddenly—without stopping to think whether it were right or wrong—he made up his mind that he would go and see for himself if the doors of the carriages opened or shut.

At this point, we—or, more likely, a contemporary reader—might recall a 1901 British film by Robert Paul, in which a bumpkin tries to look 'behind' the screen on which he has an approaching train, and succeeds in pulling the sheet down. But Bobbie has no such problems:

No sooner thought of than done, and Bobbie found himself amongst the crowd on the platform.

Yes! Hurrah! The doors did open, and Bobbie had just stepped into the carriage, when pop! flash! and a curious feeling as though he had just 'gone out' and as suddenly been lighted again, and Bobbie found himself tearing off in the cinematograph train.

Here is an engagingly sophisticated play with what was already a cliché in 1904: the reaction of spectators to movie trains entering stations. But it also points towards the idea of cinema as a 'transport of delight', a magical means of leaving the here and now.

This is also the theme of an Edison film, *The Land Beyond the Sunset* (J. Searle Dawley), which was sponsored by the Children's Fresh Air Fund in 1912 as part of its anti-tuberculosis campaign. The film shows an ill-treated newsboy from the city slums who manages to join a day trip to the seaside. The children are told a story about a boy being saved from an evil grandmother by fairies who take him to the Land Beyond Sunset. When it is time to return to the city, the boy hides and goes to the sea shore, where he finds a boat and sets sail. The final image of him drifting alone on a shimmering sea, clutching the fairy-tale book, has a poignancy equal to anything in Andersen—and a disregard for the conventions of acceptable screen behaviour which is deeply moving even today.

It is a vivid early demonstration of cinema's ability to be both literal and intensely suggestive. For many of its hard-pressed patrons, cinema had become 'the land beyond the sunset'. This magic shadow-show had become more than merely a metaphor for human existence: it was teaching its millions of spectators 'how things looked, how things worked, how we do things ... how to feel and think'.

1 *Space and Time Machine*

The image of a train stopping at a station platform was one of the first moving pictures that audiences in Europe saw. This was the celebrated *Arrival of a Train* by the Lumières and its impact became almost immediately the stuff of legend. There were stories of spectators crying out with fear, fainting, trying to escape the locomotive that seemed about to crush them. Soon there were even films about this primal experience of cinema. In Britain, Robert Paul showed a yokel seeing his first films and running in fright from a train's moving image (*The Countryman's First Sight of the Animated Pictures*, 1901), while in America 'Uncle Josh' had the same reaction in Edwin Porter's remake for Edison.

We will never know how many early spectators were truly alarmed by approaching trains. Common sense suggests it may have been very few—and even these may have been striving for effect. However a press report of the first Lumière show in Britain in March 1896 reported that:

in common with most of the people in the front rows of the stalls, I shift uneasily in my seat and think of railway accidents.

More interesting is how quickly and widely this was taken up as *the* founding myth of cinema. One of the earliest literary reports of what watching a film was like is Maxim Gorky's account of this same film:

Suddenly there is a click, everything vanishes and a railway train appears on the screen. It darts like an arrow straight towards you— watch out! It seems as though it is about to rush into the darkness where you are sitting and reduce you to a mangled sack of skin ... and destroy this hall and this building, so full of wine, women, music and vice, and turn it into fragments and dust ...

Surely a slight exaggeration? A modern Russian historian has pointed out that Gorky saw the Lumière cinematograph in a fairground next door to what was believed to be a brothel. He also wrote a short story in which a prostitute kills herself in despair after seeing the family life she will never know on the screen—in a film which may well be that other Lumière hit, *Baby's Breakfast*.

Gorky was a writer, quick to see how suggestive the film image could be. We don't have to regard him as an objective reporter any more than we might Rudyard Kipling, eight years later in 1904, when he imagined a ship's stoker driven mad by imagining that a woman glimpsed in a film was looking for him. Both Gorky and Kipling saw beyond what was often still a primitive experience. They saw that film had at least a potential power to move and inspire.

Above:
The Countryman's First Sight of the Animated Pictures (Paul, 1901)

Opposite:
Arrival of a Train (Lumière, 1895)

The image of the train suggested to another early Russian spectator that most famous of all nineteenth-century railway experiences: the death of Anna in Tolstoy's Anna Karenina. Again, we may feel incredulous. How *could* 40 seconds of a French provincial train depositing passengers on a sunlit platform conjure up that tragic scene? But if we accept that it did for at least one spectator, this may provide an important clue about how early viewers responded to films—literally, what they saw in them.

To a large extent, they saw what they brought to them. And railways already loomed large in the common experience and folklore of the late nineteenth century. First there was the new experience of mechanical speed, both terrifying and exhilarating for those who had only known horse and wind power. Then there was, literally, a new outlook on the world as it sped past the train window. On this, opinion was sharply divided. There were enthusiasts like Victor Hugo, whose eulogy to the railway experience sounds like a description of a painting by Turner or the Impressionists:

The flowers by the side of the road are no longer flowers but flecks, or rather streaks of red or white; there are no longer any points, everything becomes a streak; the grainfields are great shocks of yellow hair ... the towns, the steeples and the trees perform a crazy mingling dance on the horizon.

And there were opponents, like the champion of the Pre-Raphaelites, John Ruskin:

The railway transmutes man from a traveller into a living parcel ... It matters not whether you have eyes or are asleep or blind, intelligent or dull, all that you can know of the country you pass is its geological structure and general clothing.

and the novelist Gustave Flaubert:

I get so bored on the train that I am ready to howl with tedium after five minutes of it. One might think it's a dog someone has forgotten in the compartment; not at all, it is me groaning ... I can do nothing with the vista offered me by the compartment window.

Feeling like a parcel, being bored, unable to choose one's neighbours—these were all familiar complaints from those who resisted the rapid spread of railways during the mid-century. They were wittily expressed by Daumier and many other graphic artists of the time.

But rail travel would soon become a universal

IMPRESSIONS DE VOYAGE EN CHEMIN DE FER.
– Voilà déjà plus de huit jours qu'il n'est pas arrive d'accident sur cette ligne ...... ça ne peut pas durer longtemps comme ça .... je suis fâché d'avoir pris ce train de plaisir !

'Impressions of Railway Travel' by Honoré Daumier (1855). 'More than a week since there was an accident on this line ... it can't be much longer ... I'm furious at having to take this excursion train'

experience, and the implications for a completely new understanding of time and space were not lost on other artists. The German poet Heinrich Heine, who lived in Paris, wrote:

What changes must now occur in our way of looking at things ... Even the elementary concepts of time and space have begun to vacillate. Space is killed by the railways and we are left with time alone ... Just imagine what will happen when all the lines to Belgium and Germany are completed and connected up. I feel as if the mountains and forests of all countries were advancing on Paris. Even now I can smell the German linden trees; the North Sea's breakers are rolling against my door.

In *Through the Looking-Glass*, the Oxford logician who called himself 'Lewis Carroll' turned the railway compartment into a satirical seminar on space, time and identity in the railway age. According to Alice's fellow-travellers, having a ticket and knowing which way she's going are more important than knowing her name and the alphabet. Unsurprisingly, Alice would rather not belong to this journey! But the journey was about to become even more fantastic than Lewis Carroll could have imagined.

From the carriage window to the screen was an easy transition. It's tempting to say that sixty years of railways had prepared people to be film spectators. Moving pictures didn't actually take you somewhere, but they could transport you in imagination to anywhere. Indeed they had definite advantages,

Through the Looking-Glass (1872) illustration by John Tenniel

being cleaner, cheaper and faster than real rail travel. The next step was as inevitable as it was ironic. Fairgrounds had long used painted roller-panoramas to simulate journeys—a famous scene in Ophuls' *Letter from an Unknown Woman* celebrates the romantic side of this entertainment—now attractions like the 'Mareorama' and Hales Tours used filmed 'windows' to re-create the travel experience by sea and rail with a new verisimilitude.

Before linking this with the Disneyland and Virtual Reality of the future, it is worth reflecting that it was also entirely consistent with half a century of Magic Lantern shows and increasingly realistic theatre spectacles. Audiences of 1896 were already quite familiar with being taken on a photographic tour by a lantern lecturer, as well as with pantomimes and melodramas which brought horses, chariots, boats and even full-size locomotives on stage.

Moving pictures, at first only in black and white, may seem to us less spectacular than many other kinds of entertainment that were available when they appeared. But they clearly offered something highly attractive, which we can only try to describe as the sense of a seeing the world in a new way—the metaphor of a journey or excursion made literal. To enhance this effect, film-makers soon realised that they could set the viewpoint itself—and hence by proxy the viewer—in motion. This first took the form of a 'panorama', which meant swivelling the camera anything up to 360° to reveal an extensive scene. Then they started to mount the camera on something already moving—and the steadiest moving platform available in 1896 was a train.

So was born the 'phantom ride' which, as its name implies, took the audience on a new kind of fairground 'ride'. Within a few years, almost every exotic railway journey, from the Alps to the American West, had yielded its share of phantom rides. But like all early subjects, their novelty was soon assimilated. The next step took a leaf out of the popular folklore of railway travel. Trains were already regarded as ideal for romantic, or even downright erotic, encounters. When Dickens was reported in the newspapers as having acted bravely in a train crash, he had in fact been travelling incognito with his alleged mistress Nelly Ternan and heroism seemed the best subterfuge.

Now film-makers started offering their customers short interludes, often titled *A Kiss in the Tunnel*, to splice into the over-familiar phantom rides. Some of these were conventional 'boy kisses girl' tableaux, but others involved the girl switching places with her black maid, or an older woman deftly putting a baby's bare bottom between herself and her amorous neighbour. A 1906 film by Billy Bitzer, *Grand Hotel to Big Indian*, combines a spectacular phantom ride with a comedy scene of fighting for seats in the train. Fiction had arrived in film, rather as the 'railway library' of popular fiction had emerged to fill the tedium of train journeys twenty years earlier.

Railway-inspired fiction was also topical and violent. The crash that Dickens and Ternan survived was an ever-present danger of early rail travel. Collisions and derailments were commonplace; and the resulting drama found its way on to the stage in

A Daring Daylight Burglary
(Mottershaw, 1903)

'sensation' shows like *The Whip* at Drury Lane. Film offered a more realistic way of satisfying this rather morbid public appetite for disaster, and the genre flourished in the early years of the century. Some disaster films used model trains, but others recorded the spectacular result of trains being run deliberately into one another, as in Edison's graphically titled *Railroad Smash-Up* of 1904.

While films like these no doubt appealed to an atavistic delight in witnessing disaster—at a safe distance—they may also have satisfied a new fascination with machinery, and perhaps helped exorcise a fear of its power. Kipling and Wells were only the best-known of many writers who explored this ambivalent attitude to machines in fiction at the turn of the century. It has been called an 'operational aesthetic', growing out of the wide interest in how powerful and mysterious new technologies worked;

and film was ideally suited to satisfy it, by being able to show, not just describe, the new miracles of engineering.

But what kind of action? The last decades of the nineteenth century had seen a growth in 'sensation' material, not only on stage but also in popular novels and magazines. And one important element in this new popular culture was the role of 'new technology' in crime and its punishment. Early film producers soon recognised the advantage they had over other media in showing the modern face of crime. And in 1905 two British companies produced films based on the life and death of Charles Peace, a notoriously violent English thief whose exploits, before and after capture, had made him a popular anti-hero.

The only one of these to survive is by William Haggar, a Welsh travelling showman who started producing to supply his own popular presentations. It deals with Peace's career in a way that generally follows the traditions of the waxworks tableau and the lurid *Illustrated Police News* style of sensational illustration—until the episode of Peace's escape from police custody by jumping out of a moving train suddenly gives the film a new urgency.

Although Frank Mottershaw's version of the same story for the Sheffield Photo Company is unfortunately lost, their catalogue makes special mention of 'the Sensational Leap from the Train'. Two

The Great Train Robbery
(Porter, 1903)

years earlier, in *A Daring Daylight Burglary*, Mottershaw had already featured the burglar escaping from police pursuit by jumping on board a passing train—only to be captured by a message being telegraphed to the next station. There seems no reason to doubt the Sheffield Photo Company catalogue's claim that the film 'creates unbounded applause and enthusiasm'. And its success surely owed something to the 'operational' appeal of the unexpected railway-plus-telegraph climax to the chase.

It was this brisk and exciting film that led Mottershaw to approach the most dynamic British distributor of the time, who was actually an American, Charles Urban. Urban bought the film outright and promptly sold it to America, where Edison distributed it under the new title *Daylight Robbery*. Within months one of Edison's exployees, Edwin Porter, had taken Mottershaw's example even further in what would become one of the first major international successes, *The Great Train Robbery*. Porter's film had the undoubted advantage over Mottershaw of a 'Western' setting (though it was actually shot in New Jersey), a gallant heroine and a swaggering band of desperados. But the core of his film is the appealing conjunction of a mighty locomotive and the telegraph, here given their full due as the very mechanism of the plot.

The Wind in the Willows (1908), illustration by Ernest H. Shepard

Trains were established technology; they ran on rails and transported the masses, according to a timetable. The final years of the old century saw the emergence of a radical challenge to this predictable, conformist means of travel. After German engineers developed the internal combustion engine in the 1880s, the motor car soon became an attractive personal alternative to the enforced collectivity of the railway. Motor cars not only allowed brave individualists to 'go off the rails'; they also fostered an enthusiasm for speed as a new and soon addictive sensation. Kenneth Grahame caught this new spirit at the beginning of the new century in the bedtime stories for his son which eventually became *The Wind in the Willows*. Once behind a wheel of a car, Mr Toad becomes a true 'demon driver':

As if in a dream he found himself seated somehow in the driver's seat … and as if in a dream all senses of right and wrong, all fear of obvious consequences became suspended. He increased his pace and as the car devoured the street and leapt forth on the high road through the open country, he was only conscious that he was Toad once more, Toad at his best and highest, Toad the terror, the traffic queller, the Lord of the lone trail, before whom all must give way or be smitten into nothingness and everlasting night.

Significantly, almost all the early films that feature motor cars show them as dangerous and destructive. Cecil Hepworth's *How It Feels to Be Run Over* (1900) has a car head straight towards the camera and, according to his catalogue, it 'dashes full into the spectator, who sees "stars" as the picture comes to an end'. What we actually see is a black screen (Toad's 'nothingness'?), with animated exclamation marks and, presumably, the victim's last words: 'Oh dear, mother will be pleased'. This ironic comment on the danger that early motoring seemed to threaten is taken further in another Hepworth film of the same year, *Explosion of a Motor Car*. Here the 'explosion' (achieved by the stop-action device of cutting from a car to a puff of smoke in the same location) is followed by a Grand Guignol shower of severed limbs which rain down on a stolid policeman.

Georges Méliès' more extended *The Paris–Monte Carlo Run in Two Hours* (1905) was originally made as a series of interludes for the Folies-Bergère, but in its surviving form it shows a reckless automobile race across France, with someone or something being knocked over by a car in every scene. Motoring—at least on film—was becoming synonymous with irresponsibility.

It was also a symbol of modernity. The Italian Futurist Manifesto of 1909 set out to shock by rubbishing traditional art and aesthetics:

We affirm that the world's magnificence has been enriched by a new beauty, the beauty of speed. A racing car whose bonnet is adorned with great pipes ... a roaring car that seems to ride on grapeshot is more beautiful than the *Winged Victory of Samothrace*.

Left:
How It Feels to Be Run Over
(Hepworth, 1900)

Below:
The Paris–Monte Carlo Run in Two Hours
(Méliès, 1905)

The ? Motorist
(Paul, 1906)

One early film in particular, Robert Paul's oddly-titled *The ? Motorist* (1906), could almost be a visualisation of Toad's—or the Futurists'—automobile fantasies of omnipotence. It starts with a car running over a policemen, who 'collects the pieces of himself' and gives chase. The car then runs up the side of a building and takes off over the rooftops before heading into space and briefly driving around the ring of Saturn, like some celestial roundabout. When it returns to Earth, it falls into the midst of a Court, only to drive straight out and, just as its passengers are about to be caught, it turns into an innocent cart. But when the pursuers give up, it turns back into a car and escapes.

How are we to interpret this elaborate fantasy? Paul's detailed though deadpan catalogue description offers no clue. The basic theme of reckless motoring, together with the idea of the car 'taking off' and the chaotic courtroom, might suggest some link with *The Wind in the Willows*, but this was not published until two years later. There is however one contemporary literary reference to the film, recently pointed out by Yuri Tsivian. This appears in a 1907 essay by the leading Russian Symbolist Andrei Bely, who enthusiastically embellishes the film's action and draws from it the moral that 'walls and peaceful domesticity cannot protect us from the arrival of the unknown'. Reading this (and the other Russian material gathered by Tsivian) suggests that, almost from the beginning of cinema, it was possible for films which had no avant-garde pretensions to strike a significant chord—to express in images what could not yet be said to a wide public.

Inevitably, the exhilarating experience of motoring would be compared with that of watching a film. The French writer Octave Mirbeau (whose scandalous *Diary of a Chambermaid* was later filmed by both Renoir and Buñuel) linked the two in his 1908 evocation of 'the mind of modern man':

Everywhere life is rushing insanely like a cavalry charge, and it vanishes cinematographically, like trees and silhouettes along a road.

Both motoring and cinema offered the satisfaction of seeing the world 'whizz by': they suggest a detachment from means and consequences—Toad's sense of 'fulfilling his instincts, living his hour, reckless of what might come to him'.

Louis Lumière

Louis Lumière, right, with Auguste

Like Edison, Louis Lumière had little long-term interest in cinema. But the sheer scale and quality of his brief career in movies—from 1895 to 1900—provided a foundation for almost everyone else.

Louis (born 1864) and Auguste (born 1862) were the sons of a successful photographic manufacturer, Antoine Lumière. Louis showed early promise when he developed a new dry-plate process in 1881 which greatly boosted his father's Lyons-based business. When Antoine bought an Edison Kinetoscope in 1884, Louis started work with his brother to overcome its limitations. They patented the resulting combined camera and projector, the Cinématographe, in February 1895, and demonstrated it to professional gatherings in March and June, before the famous public show in Paris on 28 December, organised by Antoine.

The first 'views' taken by Louis in 1895 were demonstration pieces, but the composition of *Leaving the Factory*, *The Waterer Watered*, *Arrival of a Train*, *Baby's Breakfast*, *Boat Leaving the Harbour* shows a sensibility unique among the pioneers—an instinctive grasp of how to create scenes that stand endless re-viewing. However, Louis was responsible for less than fifty of the 2,113 items in the Lumières' largest (1903) catalogue. The rest were taken by roving operators like Promio, Doublier and Mesguich.

Although Louis Lumière headed the film section of the 1900 Paris Exposition, personally shooting a series of 70mm. subjects for large-screen presentation, this seems to have been the climax of his involvement with moving pictures—apart from a brief excursion into three-dimensional film in 1937. The Lumière company ceased film production in 1903, and Louis subsequently concentrated on the Autochrome colour process. He died in 1948.

R. W. Paul

Robert William Paul (1869–1943) spent only fifteen years actively involved with moving pictures, but from 1896–1900 he was the most important figure in Britain and possibly in Europe. In late 1894, he was asked, as an established scientific instrument maker, to copy Edison's Kinetoscope. In 1895, when Edison refused to supply films, Paul developed a camera (with Birt Acres) and a projector; in early 1896 he became the first English exhibitor, supplier (to Méliès among others) and producer.

Paul was interested in more than technology, judging from the early patent application inspired by Wells' 'Time Machine' and his varied production output. After the celebrated *'Persimmon' Derby*, and a *Rough Sea* which was the hit of Edison's first screening, he commissioned a travelogue sequence, *A Tour Through Spain and Portugal*, before moving to saucy comedy with *The Soldier's Courtship* (1896) and *Come Along, Do!* (1898), in which a wife hustles her husband past nude statues in a gallery. *The Last Days of Pompeii* (1897) was a pioneering literary 'adaptation'.

In 1899 Paul built an elaborate studio in Muswell Hill, North London, which enabled him to launch a new specialisation in trick films, starting with *The Human Flies* and rising in complexity through *The Haunted Curiosity Shop* (1901) to *The ? Motorist* (1906), which was directed by the trick film specialist Walter Booth. He was also one of the first to send a cameraman to South Africa to satisfy intense public interest in the Boer War.

Paul's commitment to film began to wane around 1906, although he released Britain's first *Biblical Scenes* in 1908. In 1910 he sold all his moving picture interests to return full-time to his original profession of instrument making.

The Futurists saw cinema as an essential part of the kind of spectacle they thought apt for the new world of urbanism and mechanised travel:

the cinema enriches the variety theatre with an incalculable number of visions and otherwise unrealisable spectacles ... battles, riots, horse races, automobile and aeroplane rallies, trips, journeys, depths of the city ...

If cinema seemed like an extension of the experience of rail and motor travel, it also suggested to its first viewers a mastery of the other elements—and one that again almost coincided with the technological achievement of this modern mastery.

Sea travel and transport had already been revolutionised by steam engines and iron construction. World trade—and warfare—now depended on fast and increasingly reliable worldwide navigation. Immigration, especially from Europe to the Americas, was about to benefit likewise. The next frontier to be conquered was the world beneath the sea. There were obvious military reasons to develop undersea warships which could attack without warning and provide clandestine intelligence. But there seems to have been another impulse behind the late-nineteenth-century fascination with the submarine world, which perhaps stemmed from the fact that it was another world, as yet largely unexplored and potentially a place of marvels. A scientifically believable version of the ancient myth of Atlantis, the land buried beneath the ocean.

Inevitably, it was Jules Verne's popular tale of the power-mad submariner Captain Nemo, in *20,000 Leagues Under the Sea*, that inspired the first of many submarine adventures on film. As with the railway experience, watching a film suggested an obvious analogy: the screen as a porthole, through which weird and threatening sea-monsters could be safely observed.

Even more tantalising than mastery of the seas was the conquest of the air. Balloons had already given a foretaste of what flight would feel like and as early as 1858 the French pioneer photographer Nadar used a balloon to take the first aerial photograph—a view of Paris from 520 metres. Soon this novelty was all the rage and by 1863 the popular essayist Oliver Wendell Holmes could use it as a welcome distraction from Matthew Brady's harrowing photographs of the American Civil War battlefields:

It is a relief to soar away from the contemplation of these sad scenes and fly in the balloon which carried Messrs King and Black in their aerial photographic excursion ... One of their photographs is lying before us. Boston as the eagle and the wild goose see it is a very different object from the same place as the solid citizen looks up at its eaves and chimneys.

Meanwhile the indefatigable Nadar had formed a Society for Aerial Locomotion and in that same year 1863 built a huge balloon, called 'The Giant', for a highly publicised ascent from the middle of Paris. On board were crates of champagne, food, guns, several

celebrities—and an African, to interpret in case they came down in the Dark Continent. It sounds like something out of Verne—and in fact the still unknown Jules Verne was not only a friend of Nadar and secretary of his society, but also published his first popular novel, *Five Weeks in a Balloon*, to coincide with Nadar's publicity stunt, thereby launching his own career as the century's great scientific romancer.

Heavier than air flying machines were still poised on the brink of success when cinema appeared: Adler had managed a short flight in France in 1890 before the Wright brothers achieved their historic 'first' in 1903. However, thanks to the magic of cinema, audiences could anticipate a successful solution to this challenge and experience the sensation of flight before it was actually available.

In Ferdinand Zecca's 1901 film, *The Conquest of the Air*, the film-maker himself cheerfully straddles a machine with a cigar-shaped body, bicycle pedals, bat-wings and a ship's wheel, while soaring over Paris. The technique which made possible this stunning anticipation of the future was simple, and already familiar to photographers. It involved first filming the actor in front of a blank sheet with only the upper part of the frame exposed. The film strip was then rewound in the camera and the lower part exposed in a panoramic shot of Paris, taken from the heights of Belleville. The result was a dazzling new

Original illustration for Jules Verne's
The Clipper of the Clouds (1887)

experience—like a panorama in which we, the audience, have the sensation of flight. It was to be the forerunner of many such imaginative experiences during the coming century—culminating in Cinerama, Todd-AO and IMAX.

Zecca's film was remade for Edison in the following year as *The 20th Century Tramp*, once again taking two very different recent technological successes, the airship and the bicycle, and combining them in a fantasy vehicle that confidently anticipated the era of personal mobility. A British film *Rescued in Mid-Air* (1906) added electric power and bird-like flapping wings to another prototype aeroplane—and built its plot around the lady victim of an automobile accident who uses her parasol as a parachute.

Already the cinema was becoming a laboratory for the twentieth-century imagination. For even while much effort and ingenuity was needed to achieve a short controlled flight several feet above the ground, many *fin-de-siècle* imaginations had already soared far from earth to the Moon and beyond. Verne and Wells may be the best-known today, but every country had its interplanetary visionaries. And film-makers soon followed them, first with tongue-in-cheek comedies and satires like Georges Méliès' *Journey to the Moon*, and later with more technologically plausible—yet still mythic—conceptions.

Meanwhile Verne's steady stream of futuristic tales—*Journey to the Centre of the Earth*, *From the Earth to the Moon*, *20,000 Leagues Under the Sea*, *The Clipper of the Clouds* and *The Floating Island*—strained at the limits of what was technologically feasible and imaginable. They took the reader on fantastic journeys through the air, under the earth and sea, and into space. They had thrilling endings, with disaster barely averted and families miraculously reunited. They explored the fantasies and anxieties of a generation which feared the power it had unleashed. And, of course, they were educational, with plots that often revealed the paradoxes of travelling far and fast—as when Phileas Fogg finds he's 'gained' a day on his journey round the world by crossing the International Date Line.

Space and time were becoming linked in the popular mind, even before science took up the theme. Verne's heroes get ahead of themselves, or travel beyond the end of the map; just as Rider Haggard's explorers in *She* escape from civilisation into the seductive fantasy of eternal youth. What these and many other popular artists created was a cinematic vision before the invention of moving pictures, a space and time machine of the imagination. In this, they joined Zola, Dickens, Tolstoy, Turner, Degas, Wagner and those others who also anticipated the aesthetics of cinema. For they were the first to use the close-up, slow-motion, a moving viewpoint, cross-cutting, the physical

sensation of speed and the drama of darkness and light. They, rather than the many local inventors of the camera and the projector, were the pioneers of cinema as a new kind of experience. All that remained was for reality to catch up with fiction, which it started to do in 1895 as a new industry emerged.

The Lumières were still perfecting their Cinématographe when H. G. Wells published 'The Time Machine', the first in a series of scientific fantasies which would lead to him being dubbed 'the English Jules Verne' (a title he detested!). Wells' Time Traveller patiently explains to a group of sceptical friends who represent a cross-section of society, how 'scientific people ... know very well that Time is only a kind of Space'. He goes on to give examples: a series of photographs of a man taken at different ages, and a barometer record of fluctuating air pressure over a period of time. But his guests are not convinced. One is a Psychologist, who sums up the 'great difficulty':

You *can* move about in all dimensions of Space, but you cannot move about in Time.

The arguments that the Time Traveller uses to persuade his listeners that it is possible—such as mentally 'jumping back in time'—are in fact similar to the theory of consciousness and memory that the French philosopher Henri Bergson was then developing. Bergson drew a distinction between objective and subjective experiences of time. One of his examples compared the objective, measurable time that a lump of sugar takes to dissolve in a glass of water with the 'time of impatience or desire' of someone waiting to drink the sweetened water. Opposed to the prevailing climate of scientific materialism, Bergson insisted on the importance of intuition and 'real', rather than habitual or willed memory. Bergson's theories were to become more widely known through their influence on Proust's great sequence of novels, *In Search of Lost Time*, which amounts to the sustained exploration of a life and an epoch by means of Bergson's 'subjective time'.

But all this still lay in the future in 1895, when Wells' cunningly persuasive story appeared. One of its readers was Robert Paul, a London scientific instrument maker who was already involved in the infant moving picture business. According to some accounts, Paul contacted Wells to invite his collaboration. At any rate, he filed a preliminary Patent application in October 1895 for:

A novel form of exhibition whereby the spectators have presented to their view scenes which are supposed to occur in the future or past, while they are given the sensation of voyaging upon a machine through time ... The mechanism consists of platforms for the spectators, with an opening which is directed towards a screen upon which the views are presented ...

Cecil Hepworth

The most committed of the British pioneers, Cecil Hepworth (1874–1953) came to moving pictures through Magic Lantern entertainment. As the son of a popular lantern lecturer, he had assisted with shows from childhood and started touring his own mixed slide and film show in 1896. In the following year, he published the first manual on moving pictures, *Animated Photography*, and in 1898 began making films for Charles Urban, newly arrived in London to manage what would become the Warwick Trading Company.

Hepworth's first industrial move was to set up a laboratory in 1899, with the continuous development machinery he had invented. A studio followed in 1903. By 1900 he was releasing a hundred titles annually. Hepworth was as much a producer as a film-maker and many of the famous films attributed to him were actually the work of associates—Percy Stow until 1904; then Lewin Fitzhamon, who co-directed Hepworth's most celebrated hit, *Rescued by Rover* (1905), and such inventive comedies as *The Other Side of the Hedge* (1905) and *That Fatal Sneeze* (1907).

By 1911, Hepworth's was the only British company able to compete with the appeal of imported films. He pioneered widespread poster publicity for the loyal actors who became Britain's first stars. Realising the need for longer features, he returned to directing in 1914, and even launched a short-lived US agency to sell his and other British films. But compared with American product, Hepworth's seemed tame and by 1920 he was in financial difficulty. A final bid to expand and remake his 1916 success *Comin' Thro' the Rye* failed, and after bankruptcy in 1924, the disillusioned Hepworth left the mainstream industry.

Edwin S. Porter

For five years, Edwin Porter (1869–1941) was the mainstay of Edison's film production company and so at the centre of a crucial transition from simple 'moving pictures' to narrative film. What brought him there was an early talent for machinery allied to artistic leanings. After many casual jobs, his electrical skills from the US Navy led to a job in 1896 with Edison's first projector agents. For the next four years he built and operated projectors, before a workshop fire in 1900 took him to Edison's company. Given the task of improving their projector, he soon became a cameraman-director.

Porter's first one- and two-shot films, such as *Kansas Saloon Smashers*, about women prohibitionists, and his Roosevelt satire, *Terrible Teddy, the Grizzly King* (both 1901), fitted what Musser has called the 'visual newspaper' style of early American cinema and gave little hint of what was to come.

From *Jack and the Beanstalk* (1902), through *The Life of an American Fireman* and *Uncle Tom's Cabin*, to his most famous film *The Great Train Robbery* (all 1903), can be traced Porter's discovery of how to link scenes and thereby create true screen drama. He had many English and French models to copy, but these were a breakthrough for American film-making.

Porter was never again in the vanguard. Except when inspired by technical challenges, like the aerial fantasy of *The Dream of a Rarebit Fiend* (1906), he was considered at best competent, and often clumsy. After leaving Edison in 1909, he took senior production posts with a series of new independent companies, but in 1915 Porter returned to his first enthusiasm—projectors—which occupied the rest of his working life.

After starting the mechanism, and a suitable period having elapsed, representing a number of centuries, during which the platforms may be in darkness [the audience will see] a hypothetical landscape; slide or slides traversed horizontally, containing objects such as a navigable balloon required to traverse the scene; slides or films representing living persons and their natural motions ... from made up characters performing on a stage; coloured, darkened or perforated slides used to produce the effect of sunlight, darkness, moonlight, rain, etc.

The illusion of travelling in time would be enhanced by a pretence that the spectators had 'overshot' into the past, before the Conductor would return them to the present to end the show.

This 'time machine' was never constructed, but moving pictures would soon make it a reality. And within months of filing his patent, Paul found himself one of the leading suppliers in this new industry. His surprise was probably no greater than that of the Lumière family. Antoine Lumière and his sons Louis and Auguste had built up the largest photographic business in France, employing 300 workers at their Lyons factory. Like Paul, they were first drawn into moving pictures by Edison's Kinetoscope, which prompted Louis to develop the Cinématographe, and by mid-1895 the new invention fully preoccupied the family.

Although the Lumière equipment and catalogue were devoted overwhelmingly to recording 'actuality',

even these sober manufacturers were not immune to the fashion for time-play. One of the their early films records *The Demolition of a Wall*, in which we see Auguste supervising workmen on their estate. But apparently this film was also routinely shown backwards as well as forwards. Even today, there is something eerie about seeing a heap of rubble spring up and magically form itself into a standing wall. However much we know that it is a simple trick, a mere by-product of the film process, it none the less remains a startling reminder that moving pictures quite literally made time travel a spectator sport.

There were many reasons why time should preoccupy the late nineteenth century. One was that objective, universal time was still a relatively new concept. Hitherto time had been local, regulated by custom and by church and town clocks as much as by precision instruments. Neighbouring communities could and often did have different time regimes, to which travellers adapted. But as the railways stretched out across countries and continents, passengers were confused by frequent changes of local time over a long journey, and railway companies could not publish reliable timetables. A 'reform of time' was clearly needed.

So began the series of national and international agreements which led to an orderly progression of twenty-four equal time zones measured from the prime meridian at Greenwich. Where time had been 'local' and approximate, it was now global and its standardisation was further assured by telegraphy. And as industrialisation and bureaucracy drew increasing numbers of people from the country to the city, the factory whistle and the time clock ruled ever more lives. The scientific study of work 'efficiency' began in America in the 1880s and eventually led to new forms of factory organisation and the characteristic assembly line of twentieth-century production.

By 1900, time had become a commodity. It might be invisible, but it could have immense value—a trend already satirised as early as 1872 in the railway sequence of *Through the Looking-Glass*, where the Guard's time is said to be 'worth a thousand pounds a minute'. Like money, it could be saved and spent; it could be squeezed and stretched. Thanks to recent inventions, it could be collected—in the form of photographs, phonograph records, piano rolls—and now moving pictures.

Was it mere coincidence that trains, timekeeping and moving pictures all came together at the turn of the century to create a new image of time, a new sense of its varied possibilities? Or was it that time itself had become problematic for all those undergoing the culture-shock of modernity, and cinema provided a space to exorcise this new anxiety?

One film of 1900 (apparently French) shows a train arriving at a station and passengers disembarking; then suddenly the whole action starts to run back to its beginning, to make an elegant palindrome. We can never know what its original spectators would have made of this 'remake' of the 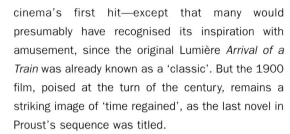 cinema's first hit—except that many would presumably have recognised its inspiration with amusement, since the original Lumière *Arrival of a Train* was already known as a 'classic'. But the 1900 film, poised at the turn of the century, remains a striking image of 'time regained', as the last novel in Proust's sequence was titled.

It would soon be followed by many more films over the next decade that treated time playfully. 'Reversing', as it became known, was found to have entertaining narrative possibilities. The Sheffield Photo Company's *An Eccentric Burglary* of 1905 worked a new variation on their established crime formula, with burglars 'flying' from the ground to an upper window, followed by the police 'sliding up' the ladder after them. Alice, of course, had discovered that the only way to go forward in Looking-Glass land was to go backwards; and that slices of cakes were handed out before they were cut in that reverse-action world.

But it was not only late Victorian fantasy and 'nonsense' literature that made free with time. Scientists too sensed that there was a revolution under way, and the power of moving pictures to provide a working model of daring new hypotheses was soon widely recognised. An American newspaper editorial of the mid-nineties made the link:

In his remarkable romance, *Lumen*, the imaginative French astronomer Flammarion, conceives of spiritual beings who, by traveling forward on a ray of light, see, with the keen vision of the spirit, all that ray of light carried

from the beginning of creation. By reversing the process and traveling in the contrary direction, they witness the events of history reversed ...

It now seems that the kinetoscope is to make this wondrous vision possible to us. Already, by allowing it to turn backwards, the actions can be seen in reverse order. The effect is said to be almost miraculous.

The breakthrough finally came in 1905 when, in order to reconcile classical physics with new discoveries in electromagnetism, Albert Einstein published the Special Theory of Relativity. This showed that time is relative to the speed of the observer and there is therefore, strictly speaking, no single universal time. Much later, in 1923, Einstein would suggest the animators and future creators of Betty Boop, Max and Dave Fleischer, to make a popular cartoon account of Relativity.

But long before Einstein's theory and name became widely known, a 'vernacular relativity' of speed and time already existed on early cinema screens. In Paul's *How to Make Time Fly* (1906), the characters' actions appear to be accelerated and slowed down according to the varying speed of a clock from which a mischievous child has taken the pendulum. *Onésime the Clockmaker*, a Gaumont comedy of 1912, has an impatient young man speed up the whole of Paris by altering the central clock so that he can quickly become old enough to inherit a legacy. As if to celebrate science's conceptual victory over the new tyranny of industrial time, cinema showed individuals taking time into their own hands.

Other new 'magical' treatments of time were also available. American Biograph's *Star Theatre* (1902) shows a Broadway theatre being demolished in two minutes, as if it were melting into the ground, by means of brief shots taken over at least a month—a technique which would soon be applied to natural history subjects. An English film of the same year, *Little Lillian, Danseuse*, features a dancer seeming to change costume at least five times in the course of the same dance. And in Porter's *City Hall to Harlem in 15 Seconds via the Subway Route* (1904) an inquisitive visitor to the subway construction site accidentally causes an explosion which shoots him like a rocket through to Harlem. American audiences in particular seemed to have unlimited enthusiasm for the new forms of transport and their ability to shrink space and time.

Talk of 'shrinking space and time' might well have recalled for an American of 1905 the new comic-strip which had just started to appear in the *New York Herald*, Winsor McCay's 'Little Nemo in Slumberland'. Each episode of Little Nemo involves an anxiety dream that threatens the innocent sleeper who then escapes by falling out of bed and waking to hear his mother's reassuring voice. Like his namesake, Verne's Captain Nemo, this young explorer of the new century's dreamscape is menaced by the powerful machinery of modern life—in one episode even by a shrinking earth, which could stand for a world already being shrunk by the new technologies of communication. And as if to close the circle, Pathé produced *A Little Jules Verne* (1907), in which a youngster in bed dreams of Verne and a series of motifs from his tales before waking in a snowstorm of feathers.

Dreams had long served artists as an excuse for fantasy and a means of exploring the forbidden and the impossible. Now early cinema inherited this tradition, and amid its early dream scenarios we find the first fantasies of flight and interplanetary travel, as well as comic dreams of wish-fulfilment and poetic justice.

It was another of McCay's dream-based strips that served as the basis for a popular Edison film of 1906, *Dream of a Rarebit Fiend*. Here a gluttonous drunk first staggers through the wildly swaying streets of New York, before being assailed by Lilliputian devils when he reaches his bed. Next his bed takes on a life of its own

Winsor McCay's
*Dreams of the
Rarebit Fiend* (1905)

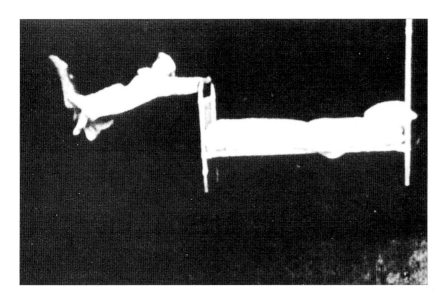

and eventually flies over the city skyline, before skewering the unhappy drunk on a steeple just before he wakes. Like a similar French film of the previous year, Gaston Velle's *Dreaming of the Moon*, this belongs to a tradition of comic fantasy at least as old as the commedia dell'arte. But film was to give such dreams a new apparatus of special effects and an added dimension of photographic realism.

No early film-maker exploited this apparatus more fully than Georges Méliès, the French pioneer who between 1902–12 created his own unique fantasy genre. Méliès was rooted in the world of nineteenth-century Paris stagecraft, based on pantomime and ballet, but also including lavish stage adaptations of Verne and the Folies-Bergère. Less didactic than the pioneers of science fiction, his films

The Dream of a Rarebit Fiend (Porter, 1906)

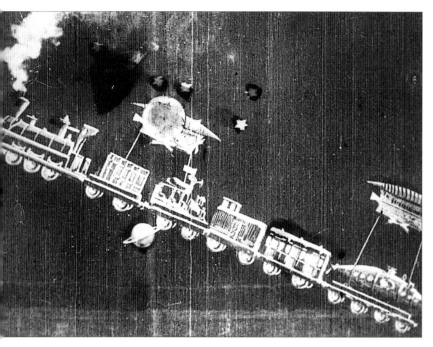

Journey Across the Impossible (Méliès, 1904)

much to their intensity as collective fantasies.

Sigmund Freud had started the work that would lead to his theory of the unconscious mind by analysing his own dreams, coincidentally in 1895. And, as a product of the railway age, he would later compare the work of psychoanalysis to a railway journey in which the patient is trying to describe the passing landscape to a listener who cannot see it. His followers who belonged to the age of cinema would see that as a more natural metaphor. In fact, like Freud, Méliès and the other pioneer film-makers belonged to a world that was already ending: the endless horizons of Verne and Rider Haggard would give way to the anxiety dreams of Wells and soon Kafka.

Méliès' masterpiece, *Journey Across the Impossible* (1904), took its title from a forgotten Verne play, but the journey undertaken by his intrepid travellers to the furthest corners of the earth and beyond into space looks more like an unguided tour of twentieth-century nightmares—an advance expedition into the dream landscape that would soon be explored by the Surrealists Max Ernst and René Magritte.

The cinema's audience was, and would largely remain, innocent of such modernism. But it soon got used to seeing 'impossible journeys' of all kinds, including travel to the moon and planets. Increasingly these seemed not only possible, but inevitable. It began to feel as if they had already happened in the realistic fantasy of cinema, so that when real space-flight was finally achieved, it seemed to many like a poor copy of the unreal thing.

evoke the dreams, nightmares and fantasies of the *fin-de-siècle* imagination rather than trying to predict what might happen in reality, as did Verne and, increasingly, Wells.

Many of Méliès' films start as journeys and expeditions, but they invariably turn into fantasy and paradox. His motorists, balloonists, undersea explorers and space travellers find themselves in mythic realms. Can we see in Méliès' knowing, seductive fantasies a commentary on the theme of 'progress'—a popular revelation of its secret fears and hopes? There are, of course, complex links between journeys in reality and fantasy or dream. And the fact that dreams of flight and penetrating the unknown were about to become reality no doubt owed

Ferdinand Zecca

Coming from the popular entertainment tradition of the Paris 'singing café', Ferdinand Zecca (1864–1947) was ideally placed to guide Pathé's production during its first decade as the world's most successful film company.

After two early films for Gaumont, *The Misadventures of a Calf's Head* and *The Dangers of Alcoholism* (both 1898–9), Zecca joined Pathé in 1901 and soon became the company's most prolific director, before he was appointed its general manager in 1910. From the start, he aimed at a direct, sensational appeal—ideally suited to the fairground exhibitors who were Pathé's earliest customers. His first notable film, *The Story of a Crime* (1901), followed the style of popular crime illustration, complete with painted backdrops. Another, *The Conquest of the Air* (1901), showed Zecca waving from a bird-like bicycle that floats magically above the Paris skyline.

Working with Pathé's animation specialist, Segundo de Chomón, Zecca used fantasy in many of his films and has often been accused, perhaps unfairly, of stealing from Méliès. However, his two versions of *The Life and Passion of Jesus* (1902–4, with Nonguet; 1907, with de Chomón) show a distinctively robust treatment of this supernatural story.

Burch detects a populist support for rebels and underdogs in films like *The Incendiary, Revolution in*

Russia (both 1905) and *The Nihilist* (1906), while other historians have been more inclined to see Zecca as a shrewd judge of his customers' tastes. After 1910, his role was confined to supervision and in 1913 he was sent overseas to supervise Pathé's US branch. Back in France after the war, Zecca headed Pathé-Cinéma, which handled equipment and processing, until his retirement in 1939.

2 *Tales from the City*

M oving pictures were still a novelty in the Paris of 1897. So a programme specially for children must have seemed a good idea to the organisers of the annual Spring Charity Bazaar. The site was a vacant area near the Champs-Elysées and, in keeping with that year's sixteenth-century theme, a large striped marquee was erected for the film show, entered through a turnstile. The capacity audience that gathered on the afternoon of 4 May included many prominent society figures associated with the bazaar as well as the children. Although film-shows at this early date were already attracting a wide social cross-section of the curious and the idle, these were almost certainly the most distinguished viewers to date.

Suddenly, in the midst of the show the projector's ether lamp went out. The projectionist tried to relight it, but his efforts led to an explosion and within seconds the marquee was a blazing inferno. The final death count was 140, with many choked and trampled as they tried to escape through the narrow entrance. Press coverage was copious and detailed, largely because so many public figures were involved. A duel was even fought over allegations that the husband of one victim, Count Robert de Montesquiou (the model for Proust's Baron de Charlus), had saved himself at his wife's expense. The Charity Bazaar fire was the first tragedy of the film era—a terrifying reminder of how dangerous early projection could be in crowded, darkened spaces. And since a majority of screenings outside city variety theatres continued to he held in tents for some years, it undoubtedly fed anxieties about the safety of this new entertainment, which eventually led to safer projectors and strict fire safety regulations.

Yet the Charity fire does not seem to have discouraged audiences, as has often been claimed. If anything, it may have boosted them and given the new entertainment a more fashionable appeal. Within months, a giant screen was installed at a popular ice rink also on the Champs-Elysées and *le tout Paris* went to admire the 'marvellous sharpness and precision' of the Lumière films. For film-going seemed ideally suited to the last years of the nineteenth century, as they were being experienced by vast numbers of people. An early Italian comedy, *Tontolini Is Sad*, shows a distraught man trying unsuccessfully to distract himself at the theatre and the circus, before finally falling under the spell of a comedy at the cinema. The message may be self-serving, but it also confirms what actually happened between 1896 and the great wave of cinema building that started around 1908. An appetite, or a habit, was being created and this was by no means confined to the working class; and an industry emerging to feed it. Movies had become the mirror of modern life—which meant city life.

By the end of the nineteenth century, it seemed that everyone would soon be living in a city. Before long the whole world would *be* one huge extended city. This wasn't just a fantasy of professional prophets like H. G. Wells and Jules Verne: it followed directly from the experience of the previous fifty years. The cities of Europe and America—Paris, London, New York, Chicago—were growing like organisms or machines out of control, doubling their

Charity Bazaar fire, Paris, 1897

size every decade. There seemed no reason why this should end. E. M. Forster's story 'The Machine Stops' already foresaw in the early years of the new century the whole of humanity living in physical isolation, while fully linked to one another by interactive sound and vision.

Yet until the explosion of the new metropolis, most cities still had the narrow, crooked streets of the Middle Ages. As the new city dwellers poured in, these were swept away by bold new building plans. The most dramatic was Haussmann's replanning of Paris in the 1860s. Now streets were straight and planned, buildings were elegant and designed, and beneath the streets there was also a new network of sewers, pipes and railways—a new underworld, which would soon inspire the next generation of storytellers. For those who had grown up in the cosy old-style city, life would never be the same again. The Goncourt brothers kept a diary of life in Paris during these upheavals.

> Our Paris ... the Paris of the way of life of 1830 to 1848, is passing away. Its passing is not material but moral. Social life is going through a great evolution ... The interior is passing away. Life turns back to become public ... I am a stranger to what is coming ... as I am to these new boulevards ... which no longer smack of Balzac [but] of London, of some Babylon of the future.

For true connoisseurs of city life, the street became a new kind of 'interior', a place where they felt at home.

In that same year, the French poet Charles Baudelaire spoke eloquently on behalf of these new urban idler:

> For the perfect *flâneur*, it is an immense joy to set up house in the heart of the multitude, amid the ebb and flow of movement, in the midst of the fugitive and the infinite. To be away from home and yet to feel oneself everywhere at home ... to be at the centre of the world and yet to remain hidden from the world. He enters into the crowd as if it were an immense reservoir of electrical energy. Or we might liken him to a mirror as vast as the crowd itself; or a kaleidoscope gifted with consciousness ... He is an 'I' with an insatiable appetite for the 'non-I', at every instant rendering it in pictures more living than life itself.

Baudelaire's celebration of being alone in a crowd reads today like a remarkable anticipation of the moving picture spectator, for whom the cinema would become a novel way of being 'at home' in the modern metropolis and continuing to indulge the *flâneur*'s instincts. The spread of covered arcades in Europe developed the idea of an 'interiorised' city, and it was often in these that cinemas were located—early ancestors of the modern American shopping-mall movie theatres.

Baudelaire did not live long enough to experience cinema, but the Russian poet Aleksandr Blok was an early film addict, and he wrote in a letter of 1904 about how cinemas attracted people like him:

Billy Bitzer

Billy Bitzer (1872–1944) entered cinema history as the Sancho Panza to D. W. Griffith's Don Quixote. One sentence from Bitzer's memoirs has often been singled out to characterise their sixteen-year relationship as cameraman and director: 'What Mr Griffith saw in his mind we put on the screen.'

No doubt this was true, for they had grown together through the hundreds of Biograph shorts and had developed a unique rapport by the time Griffith persuaded Bitzer to leave Biograph in 1913 'to make the greatest pictures ever made'. Fifteen years later, both would know the bitterness of being cast aside by an industry they had helped create.

Gottlob Wilhelm 'Billy' Bitzer had trained as a silversmith before he joined the Magic Introduction Company in New York in 1894, just as the Kinetoscope appeared. A year later, Bitzer's employer in the novelty company became a partner in the American Mutoscope Company, started by Edison's former assistant Dickson, and Bitzer found himself pressed into service as operator of their clumsy Biograph projector at the press launch in October 1896.

He was soon also their chief cameraman, filming the future President McKinley, warships in the Cuban war, the prize-fights which were popular early film subjects, and 'the picturesque West'. Cameramen had no

Billy Bitzer, left, with D. W. Griffith

directors at this time, so when the market demanded fiction Bitzer, like Porter, became an inadvertent director. The Library of Congress Paper Print Collection has about 400 of the titles he made between 1900 and 1908. These, even before his sublime and inventive collaborations with Griffith, are the record of a new folk art's birth.

He was only saved from destitution in the thirties by the Museum of Modern Art film department inviting him to help identify films and write about his early experiences.

Arturo Ambrosio

Although there were Italian patents for moving picture equipment as early as 1895, no immediate steps seem to have been taken to realise these or make films in Italy, other than by Lumière operators—Promio's 1896 tracking shot from a Venetian gondola was an early hit. The founder of Italian cinema was a Turin optical merchant, Arturo Ambrosio (1869–1960), who started making actualities in 1904 and built his own studio in the following year.

Ambrosio's versatile cameraman Giovanni Vitrotti travelled widely around Italy filming what would elsewhere be called 'interest' films about local industries (wine, tomatoes, vermouth) and customs. Meanwhile, Ambrosio had embarked on comedies in 1906 with Ernesto Vaster, and also developed an early relationship with Pathé which gave him access to their comedies.

In 1908 Ambrosio moved ambitiously into full-scale fiction with two spectacular films directed by Luigi Maggi, *The Count of Montecristo* and *The Last Days of Pompeii*. The latter helped create an international market for Italian spectacles of the ancient world, which were soon also provided by Ambrosio's Turin rival Giovanni Pastrone and by the Roman company Cines. Ambrosio's strategy was to seek partners abroad, and in 1910 he signed the first of several such agreements with the Russian firm of Thiemann and Reinhardt. The Russians were loaned Vitrotti and in exchange Ambrosio received a supply of exotic documentaries and Russian literary adaptations.

In 1911, Ambrosio took another bold step forward when he made an agreement with the leading Italian poet and dramatist Gabriele D'Annunzio for exclusive film rights on all the writer's work, quickly producing four adaptations in the same year. Although the international market for Italian spectacle declined after the First World War, Ambrosio continued as a major producer into the 1920s.

Yesterday I set off for your place [but] I suddenly saw that cinema on Liteinaya Street and I went in and watched the pictures for about an hour ... There is a kind of city mystery here, like hidden ambushes ... The thing to do is to trick yourself into slipping past them.

And what did those 'ambushed' in this way see? The very first moving picture subjects were often simply the city streets from which the audience had just come. The marvel was that this kaleidoscope of action could be captured in all its detail and replayed in an eerie silence. The Lumières filmed their own workers pouring out of the factory gate in 1895: the very first moving image of the new industrial workforce, who would soon become cinema's voracious consumers. In the next year Robert Paul filmed the crowd on London's Westminster Bridge, providing a visual echo of Thomas Carlyle's first great invocation of the urban crowd—'that living flood ... of all qualities and ages'—sixty years earlier.

City scenes came later in America, due to Edison's early use of a studio for the production of his Kinetoscope subjects. But soon there were evocative scenes of American city streets, like the 1903 Biograph view of a teeming *Lower Broadway* which would inspire Martin Scorsese to restage it ninety years later for his *Age of Innocence*.

There were also street scenes from foreign cities, which for many American audiences would have been more nostalgic than 'exotic', after the great waves of immigration, especially from Europe. The rituals of arrival in the New World are recorded on film, as is the survival of traditional customs in America's immigrant communities. Picture shows not only catered for the entertainment of non-English speakers, as traditional cinema history has always claimed; they also helped keep ethnic culture alive through the import of films from 'the old country', as well as speeding the assimilation of the next generation.

It was during the years when the urban scene was first filmed that the crowd also became an object of study. The new science of sociology took shape with Durkheim's work on the alienation of modern life, LeBon's *The Crowd: A Study of the Popular Mind* and Simmel's *The Metropolis and Mental Life*. These writers all considered the crowd to be something essentially different from a mass of individuals: biological and electrical metaphors were especially common to explain its dynamics. Some believed that new mental and social types were appearing in the vast cities.

One of Simmel's themes was the city-dweller's rapid assumption of a condescending attitude towards his country cousin, the 'rube', and indeed this recurs often in turn-of-the-century American vaudeville and comic-strips, as well as cinema. *Rubes in the Theatre* (Edison, 1901) shows two countrymen over-reacting to a show and being laughed at by their neighbours, while *Rube and Mandy at Coney Island* (Edison, 1903) provides a tour of the amusement park in the company of a couple who end up stuffing themselves messily with hot-dogs. Back in the city, Biograph's *A Rube in the*

Subway shows a country hick confused by the New York subway system and having his pocket picked.

There is another 'rube' film preserved in the Library of Congress's unique Paper Print Collection, an invaluable legacy of American copyright concerns of 1895–1912. This is *Rube in an Opium Joint*, made in 1905 by D. W. Griffith's future cameraman, Billy Bitzer. It shows, bizarrely, a middle-aged couple being ushered into an opium den by an enthusiastic tour guide with a megaphone and the 'rube' being offered a pipe by one of the denizens. After a trial puff, he prefers his own pipe, but as the pair leave the other opium smokers are seen with pipes similar to his. Even by the standards of other early films which take for granted what contemporary audiences would have known this is hard to fathom. But help is at hand, when we discover that this short episode was included in a longer film, released just two weeks later as *Lifting the Lid*.

The later film starts in a busy New York street, where a bus-load of sightseers is setting off. We then join the guide with a megaphone as he anxiously shepherds a middle-aged couple through a series of low-life encounters, each arranged as studio set-pieces. First the 'rube' gets into a fight in a dance-hall, then he starts an argument with a waiter in a Chinese restaurant. Next comes the Opium Joint episode (presumably attached to the Chinese restaurant?) and finally he climbs on to the stage of a show-restaurant, as if determined to perform. The film ends back on the street, with the tour bus pulling up.

What are we to make of this? Is it a comic fantasy about how the 'rube' couple imagine the city, or a mockery of their failure to understand it—or conceivably, as in the Opium Joint scene, a celebration of their solid refusal to be shocked by urban decadence? It is difficult to choose between these interpretations without further contextual information, but *Lifting the Lid* at least suggests a more nuanced version of the basic 'rube' satire—as well as offering a tour of the kind of big-city entertainment which film could now deliver to the sticks.

Like the 'rube' the immigrant was also a figure of fun in such films as *A Gesture Fight in Hester Street* (Biograph, 1900), where two pedlars fight for the same pitch, and *Levi and Cohen, the Irish Comedians* (Biograph, 1903), in which the aspiring performers are pelted with tomatoes. National and ethnic stereotypes were commonplace. In Biograph's *Hot Mutton Pies* (1902), two boys discover to their disgust that what they have just bought from a pigtailed Chinaman are 'cat pies'; while the gruesomely comic explosion in *A Catastrophe in Hester Street* (Biograph, 1904) appears to be caused by drunken anarchists.

Almost all of these were made in studios with simple stage scenery, since the logistics of crowd control and filming did not encourage taking to the streets. But even though early films rarely showed actual cities, they can still give a much clearer insight than other media into the changing world of the city-dweller. Where no traditions existed, a new medium appealing mainly to the anonymous masses had to find subjects and ways of treating them which were immediately attractive and recognisable. So, from the random sample of films that have survived, we can trace a general shift from static to dynamic points of view; a new eroticism based on film's ability to create an anonymous intimacy; and the gradual emergence of a new mythology of crime.

The crowded street was one of the first moving picture subjects, but it had the disadvantage of being essentially static. Even when conscientiously reconstructed in the studio, as for Frank Dobson's

The Streets of New York (1905), with an elaborate choreography of encounters, fights and petty crime, the steady focus on a single corner seems to contradict the mobility of city life. From the start there had been the alternative of a moving point of view, as in Robert Paul's 1897? *On a Runaway Car Through Piccadilly Circus*, which apparently (the film is lost) used accelerated motion to convey the sense of speeding through city streets.

One subject that automatically provided this spectacle was the fire-brigade turn-out. And so, for over a decade, fire engines of all kinds—horse, steam and motor-drawn, even on sledge-runners—rushed silently across the world's screens. Initially the speed and panoply of the turn-out was the attraction, but soon this was linked with the fire rescue, following Edwin Porter's landmark film, *The Life of an American Fireman* (1903).

Fire-brigade exploits were only too common in the densely crowded new cities, and they were already well represented in other media before the arrival of moving pictures, with paintings, prints, lantern-slides and theatrical shows. There were also fire films before Porter's, but *The Life of an American Fireman* shaped and compressed the whole drama, from the firemen sliding down their poles and driving hell for leather

Fire! (Williamson, 1901)

The Rescue (1855) by
John Everett Millais

Lantern slide from
Bob the Fireman series

through city streets to the scene of the fire. Porter went on to show both the inside of the burning house, with a distraught mother and child, and the outside scene of firemen and ladders (although it seems that these were intercut for greater drama by a later hand than his in some versions of this classic film).

Alongside the fire engine's hectic passage through city streets there was the chase, which emerged early in the century as the conventions for extending action through a sequence of shots were established. Usually sparked by some misdemeanour or minor crime, though soon taking on a momentum of their own, chases were rarely set in city centres—the logistics of crowd and traffic control ruled this out—but even those filmed in the suburbs seem to have conveyed an urban dynamism. Freed from the all too real tragedy associated with fire, chases could follow a playful, fantastic logic—all for the pleasure of pursuit, never about realism or any kind of justice, other than poetic. In Cricks and Martin's *The Biter Bit* (Britain, 1909), a bag-snatcher is chased by a growing band out of the city into the countryside. Even though he resorts to a bicycle and motor car at various stages, the pursuers manage to keep up, until he finally opens the bag—and a terrier jumps out, to hold him fast until the crowd catches up.

Another British chase film, Lewin Fitzhamon's *That Fatal Sneeze* (1907), follows the same pattern of poetic justice. A man makes a boy sneeze with pepper, whereupon the boy retaliates by putting pepper all over the man's bedroom. As the man starts sneezing, he goes out into the street and his epic sneezes become increasingly destructive,

attracting ever more irate tradespeople to chase him. His last sneeze proves truly volcanic: the film image disappears and we assume that he, or perhaps even the world, has blown up. Two French chase films of 1908, *The Runaway Horse* (Louis Gasnier) and *The Pumpkin Race* (Romeo Bosetti), abandon human fugitives for, respectively, a supercharged horse with cart and a bouncing load of self-propelled pumpkins.

These innocent fantasies of urban chaos and disorder, made by artisans rather than artists, coincided almost exactly with the revolution in the arts that has come to be known as Modernism. All the creators of new forms to express a new outlook—Symbolists, Cubists, Futurists, Imagists, 'stream of consciousness' writers, atonal composers—were also, for the most part, avid film-goers. Some of them dreamed of artistic uses of film, most of which never materialised. Others became involved in cinema or drew inspiration from it in unexpected ways. Andrei Bely, for instance, was a Russian Symbolist of the same generation as Blok who wrote in 1908:

That Fatal Sneeze
(Fitzhamon, 1907)

What Happened on 23rd Street, New York City
(Edison, 1901)

Man is a cloud of smoke, he catches a cold, he sneezes and bursts ... The cinematograph reigns in the city, reigns over the earth. In Moscow, Paris, New York, Bombay, maybe at the very same hour, thousands of people see a man who sneezes and explodes. More than the preachings of wise men, the cinematograph has demonstrated to everyone what reality is.

To Bely, writing about a Russia still nervous after the failed Revolution of 1905, *That Fatal Sneeze* may have suggested a key image—the knowledge that a man may be blown up at any moment—for his great experimental novel *Petersburg*, often regarded as the 'Russian *Ulysses*'.

Meanwhile, the future author of *Ulysses* was living in Trieste in 1909 when he was persuaded that Dublin might be ready for its first high-class cinema. So Joyce reluctantly left his wife Nora to return to Ireland and prepare for the opening of 'The Volta', which was intended to show only Italian films, then becoming popular. However the real drama of this episode took place off-screen, in a remarkably frank erotic correspondence between Nora and Joyce which left its mark on his future writing. The Volta was not a success, and they were soon reunited in exile. But Joyce became fascinated by cinema: years later he wanted the pioneer of Soviet revolutionary modernism (and close friend of Bely) Sergei Eisenstein to film *Ulysses*, and his disciple Samuel Beckett planned to study screenwriting with Eisenstein.

Among the early Paris Modernists, it was the poet and critic Apollinaire, a close friend of Picasso, who first drew attention to the scandalous potential of cinema in his witty story, 'A Fine Film' (1904). This has a suave rogue, the Baron d'Ormesan, tell how he and a group of friends founded the 'International Cinematographic Company' and won an enviable reputation for the authenticity of their films—of subjects such as the French President getting dressed, the birth of a royal heir and the suicide of the Turkish prime minister—all due to bribing those responsible for guarding their masters' privacy. But the ICC wondered how to add a 'real' crime film to their repertoire. The solution lay in kidnapping a trio of innocent passers-by and inviting one, suitably disguised, to stab the other two on camera, which, according to the Baron, he did with some relish.

The resulting film is hailed as another triumph of realism. The murdered couple turn out to be adulterers; the police ignore the makers' claims of authenticity, and the ICC even manages to film the execution of another innocent party charged with the murders. This fable of rampant sensationalism, still shocking today for its urbanity, probably tells us more about attitudes to the cinema in fashionable Paris than anything other than the films themselves.

What many of these confirm is the *voyeurism* that the new medium satisfied—another of the traits that Simmel had identified in the new urban sensibility. This was less a matter of contrived 'peep-show' films like *As Seen Through a Telescope* (Smith, 1900) and *Scenes from My Balcony* (Zecca, 1901), both involving middle-aged men spying on girls with a telescope, than of discovering new erotic possibilities in the city scene itself. Two early American films demonstrate this with an apparent insouciance. Edison's *What Happened on 23rd Street, New York City* (1901) shows a young woman walking with her escort who suddenly finds her skirt lifted by the draught from a sidewalk grating—a forerunner of the celebrated image of Marilyn Monroe similarly 'surprised' in *The Seven Year Itch*. Biograph's *At the Foot of the Flatiron* (1903) takes a similar tack by placing the camera at a notoriously windy corner in New York apparently much favoured by admirers of women's ankles.

It was not only the city streets that generated a new climate of erotic opportunity; there was also the tantalising promise of what might be happening behind any impassive facade. Passion, of course, is rarely admitted, let alone allowed, in American or British films of this period. But, true to national stereotype, it formed a staple part of French cinema. Amorous encounters in the street, lovers smuggled into and out of respectable bourgeois households, and *crimes passionnels* were more common in the output of Pathé-Frères than under the strait-laced Léon Gaumont. In one striking Pathé melodrama, *For a Necklace* (1907), a man is driven to theft and ruin by his wife's insatiable desire for jewellery. In despair, he jumps from their apartment window to his death on the pavement below. The image still shocks, especially when it is followed by the wife gloating over the return of her favourite necklace with her husband's corpse laid out in the

The Story the Biograph Told (Biograph, 1904)

background. Here we can begin to see how the cinema will inherit the mantle of Zola with a distinctively modern image of depravity.

By the time moving pictures became established, other new technologies had already started a social revolution with profound implications for relations between the sexes. The telephone and the office 'typewriter', as women typists were originally known, feature in many early films which show the new dynamics of city office life. Edison's *Appointment by Telephone* (1902) starts in a brokers' office with a man making a telephone call. He then meets a woman, whom he has presumably just called, at a restaurant, but they are soon interrupted by another woman who attacks the man.

Modern infidelity is also the theme of *The Story the Biograph Told* (made by Biograph in 1904). Set again in a city office, this starts with a man demonstrating the film camera to an office boy—who then proceeds to secretly film his employer making advances to a secretary. The scene changes to a theatre, where the same man, now with his wife, is watching a film. To her dismay, the film shows the husband and secretary. In the final scene, the wife storms into the office and replaces the

female secretary with a male one. The fear that moving pictures might produce indiscreet or incriminating evidence was not uncommon at this time, but *The Story the Biograph Told* seems to crystalise a particular exhibitionist fantasy in the image of adultery writ large on the cinema screen.

Films that include the experience of watching films inevitably raise questions about the film audience of the early 1900s: where did it come from, how was it composed, and where did it gather? Traditionally, cinema has been characterised as a working-class entertainment, vulgar and undemanding, which—depending on the bias of the writer—either gradually won respectability, or succeeded in attracting a mass audience to its low cultural level. Most recent studies paint a rather different picture. The first film shows, invariably given in prestigious salons and lecture

halls, attracted a wide social spectrum. Further commercial screenings then became part of the programmes of variety theatres and music-halls, of waxworks and wintergardens, and of other established entertainment venues. They also took place at fairs and international exhibitions—the Nizhny-Novgorod Fair in Russia was where Gorky saw the Lumière debut in 1896—and at countless private screenings, which soon included presentations to royalty and heads of state.

In this first phase, moving pictures were seen as, variously, a scientific achievement, an educational experience and a 'refined' entertainment. But there was the major problem of where they could be shown regularly. Between 1896 and around 1904, many music-halls, vaudeville theatres and their equivalents in other countries became part-time cinemas as the balance between 'live' and film material in their programmes changed. Meanwhile, two other important developments were under way, neither particularly respectable, which would also contribute to shaping the cinema industry. One was the growth of touring film shows—'peep-shows', and the other a transformation of the already established amusement parlours.

Moving pictures found an early foothold in the fairgrounds of many countries. They were an ideal novelty to add to the attractions which fairs brought regularly to enliven provincial life. Soon, the touring showmen had become major investors in moving-picture equipment and presentation. From the beginning, it was showmen who controlled what audiences actually saw. They selected items from the catalogues of the producers, then decided what order they should be shown in. It was they who could turn a series of discrete 'subjects' into an extended narrative—and change the direction and meaning of the narrative by their choices. A 'Kiss in the Tunnel' dropped into a series of 'Phantom Rides' could turn them into an amorous journey. Producers might advise on what items to combine, but it was the showmen who discovered from experience what audiences understood and liked—from which it was a short step for some to become producers of films themselves.

The other early venues for regular moving picture shows were the arcade 'parlours' which had first been established in the early 1890s to exploit Edison's Phonograph, and then added his Kinetoscope, or the rival Mutoscope. These were both peep-show machines for single viewers: the Kinetoscope was electrically powered, and the Mutoscope a hand-cranked development of the 'flick book' principle. The concept was attractively modern, especially in big cities, and parlours spread rapidly to Europe and further afield. They catered for a sense of individualism and economy. The Automatic Vaudeville, in New York's Union Square, advertised itself as 'the greatest place of amusement on earth for one cent'. It was in one such Phonograph and Kinetoscope Parlour in Los Angeles in 1902 that the operator added a projector and screen behind the slot-machines. When the projected pictures proved more popular, he turned his arcade into the Electric Theatre offering 'up-to-date high class motion picture entertainment especially for ladies and children'.

The Princess Theatre in St Cloud, Minnesota in 1911, showing two Italian films

The first wave of converting buildings specifically to show films started around 1905 and is often linked with opening of the first 'Nickelodeon' in November of that year in Pittsburgh. Essentially, the nickelodeon was a shop-sized space which could seat just under 200 people on tightly-packed chairs (to avoid the theatre taxes which became due on more than 200 spectators). Within a year, there were an estimated thousand nickelodeons in American cities. Programmes ran from 8 a.m. to midnight with popular music played by a pianist as an added attraction. As the business boomed, enterprising builders began to produce ready-made frontages and cinemas began to acquire their distinctive decor. Like the fairground showmen who became producers, many of Hollywood's future tycoons, such as Adolph Zukor and Carl Laemmle, started as nickelodeon proprietors at this time.

It was at this time, too, that film exhibition acquired a low-class image. In America, nickelodeons were regarded as a the resort of the poor, the immigrant and the work-weary. In Britain, they were known as 'penny gaffs' and thought of as dirty, badly equipped and infested with pickpockets. Elsewhere there were the same complaints, as in this reminiscence of early film-going in Odessa:

A small, permanently stuffy room crowded with chairs ... some weird apparatus jealously guarded by a mysterious man whom we called 'the mechanic'. He was the one who collected the money and cranked the handle ... The audience, usually children and young people, were unrestrained; they chewed seeds and munched apples, throwing the husks and cores on the floor and at each other.

The future of moving pictures looked bleak, condemned to a downward spiral of quality and earnings. Then, quite suddenly, in 1907–8 the business of film exhibition started to move on to a new level.

Partly this was due to external pressure. Faced with a widespread backlash against the supposed 'immorality' of many films, American nickelodeons were threatened by summary closure in 1908. Early in the following year, they formed a voluntary Board of Censorship and soon exhibitors were deliberately trying to attract more 'family' and middle-class patrons. The new cinemas boasted refined names, impressive frontages, small orchestras (or the versatile new Wurlitzer organ)—and they began to show imported 'cultural' films. The same trend had already started in Britain, with theatres entirely devoted to film starting in 1907. And in France, the two major film companies Pathé and Gaumont were now locked in deadly competition, not only as international exporters of their productions, but as exhibitors.

All that was needed in this climate of upward social mobility were films to match cinema's new image. They were not long in appearing. In 1908 the French Art Film Company produced *The Assassination of the Duc de Guise* with unprecedented lavishness and attention to detail. Actors, costume and setting were all in harmony—and the producers even went so far as to commission an orchestral score from one of leading composers of the day, Camille Saint-Saëns. The Art Film Company was soon taken over by Pathé and later historians have mocked its pretensions, but it proved to be only the tip of an emerging iceberg. Everywhere producers were reaching back into history and vying with each other to scale new heights of authenticity.

Italy soon led the way with spectacular re-creations of the ancient world in *The Last Days of Pompeii* (1908) and *Nero, or the Burning of Rome* (1909), closely followed by dozens of literary classics. The impact of these was overwhelming, especially in smaller communities that had previously lacked any real cultural amenities. Cinema now brought a vivid vision, not only of distant places but of the historic past. An original American trade review of *Nero*, which was colour tinted and accompanied by a special programme brochure, evokes its impact:

> **... such a marvelous realism of effect that as we sat and watched the colored part of the film, we seemed, as it were, to hear the cries of the victims.**

The pagan decadence of Ancient Rome had given birth to militant Christianity. For audiences still deeply responsive to religious guidance, this was enough to justify more licentiousness on screen than would otherwise have been tolerated. Despite Henry Ford's notorious claim that 'history is more or less bunk', audiences throughout the world were being plunged into a vividly imagined history that soon

The Assassination of the Duc de Guise (Le Bargy, Calmette, 1908)

seemed more real than their everyday lives. What would the long-term consequences be?

In the short term, film producers almost everywhere delved into 'the classics' to satisfy a new appetite for history and culture. The Vitagraph company in America started filming Shakespeare, Dickens and Dante in 1908, while Edison concentrated on history. In Britain there were ambitious films based on Shakespeare's *Henry VIII*, *Macbeth* and *Richard III*, all made in 1911. The infant Russian industry turned quickly to Pushkin for *The Queen of Spades* and to the reign of Catherine the Great for a local Pathé art film production, *Princess Tarakanova* (both 1910) .

Films and cinemas to show them were now moving ahead in tandem. As nickelodeons and 'penny gaffs' disappeared from all but the poorest districts, there emerged a hierarchy of better appointed theatres, crowned by the most lavish in city centres, which fully justified the nickname of 'picture palaces'. Cinema decor became as fantastic as the films themselves, deliberately evoking (and mixing) classical and exotic styles. The naming of cinemas took on ever greater significance, with fashions that moved from 'Bijou' and 'Princess' to 'Rex', 'Regal' and

'Palace'. Another key development was the foyer, serving as a transit-zone between the street and the auditorium. Here, amid potted palms and theatrical furniture, spectators could adjust their fantasies to mundane reality, or vice versa.

In a country like Russia, which had only recently started to modernise, luxury cinemas could have an even more symbolic function than elsewhere. The daughter of a Siberian gold merchant had visited France and developed a sudden interest in cinema. She promptly struck a deal with Pathé to supply films for the distinctive cinemas she envisaged for St Petersburg:

These were all exact copies of Paris cinemas, with orchestras, cafés, foyers, beautiful young barmaids and usherettes. The first, called 'Just Like Paris', was situated in a cosy detached house in a courtyard off Nevsky Prospect. Outside there were two huge coloured posters of Paris ... A deep pile carpet led the public into an elegant foyer. After midnight there were performances of 'Parisian genre' (meaning pornographic) films ... put on free of charge for select members of the city authorities.

The Gaumont Palace in Paris, advertised as 'the largest cinema in the world'

In Russia, and no doubt elsewhere, luxury cinemas took over a social function previously fulfilled by the theatre and opera. They were places of private resort and assignation, with boxes for secret rendezvous, even telephones—and they had the advantage of being *darker* than other kinds of theatre!

The climax of the development of cinemas from nickelodeons to 'picture palaces' was the Gaumont Palace, opened in Paris in 1912. This provided unprecedented luxury for a mass audience—a temporary, but affordable, experience of gracious living. The cinema industry was now launched on a course that would soon enable it to shape the leisure habits of the majority of the world's population. Flagship cinemas defined the entertainment districts of cities everywhere, while smaller cinemas catered for other districts and reached out into ever-smaller towns.

Above all, cinema symbolised the appeal of 'the city'. It reflected the concerns of its majority urban audience and relayed these to far-flung rural audiences, attracting the next generation of 'rubes' who would become city-dwellers. Despite repeated moral panics, it traded on and indeed reinforced the glamour of big-city sophistication—with images of dancing, alcohol, gambling, prostitution, drugs and crime. Films were helping to create a new mythology of the city as a modern Babylon.

The Musketeers of Pig Alley
(Griffith, 1912)

The very earliest films, especially in America, were not coy about dealing with the more sordid aspects of city life and crime. In Biograph's *A Legal Hold-Up* (1902) a policeman beats up and robs a prosperous citizen in broad daylight, while no passers-by intervene. An equally shocking example from the same year is *The Girl Who Went Astray*, one of a cycle of films entitled *The Downward Path*, which shows an innocent country girl inexorably dragged into big-city vice. In this episode the girl has become a prostitute, and a pimp attacks her in the street just as her aged parents find her. And now it is a passing policeman who studiously avoids intervening.

Corruption, as implied in these and other films, was very much an American preoccupation—and of course it reflected a real and persistent struggle to square Protestant morality with aggressive capitalism. This struggle and the vigorous publicity that accompanied it gave American film producers a source of topical and often very raw material which

few Europeans could, or would have been allowed to, match. More typical of European attitudes was Gaumont's prim *The Police as They Are Represented to Us* (1908), which shows first lazy and corrupt police, only to reveal that 'in reality' they are fearless crime fighters, who daily risk injury in the line of duty.

In America, the city crime genre was to take a remarkably dynamic form. Even D. W. Griffith, who had earlier shown the city as a moral cross-roads for his pure-hearted heroines and who felt himself more of a poet and Southern gentleman than a muck-raker, was attracted by the potential of the city's criminal milieu, which also happened to be thriving around the 14th Street New York studio where he was working in 1912.

His *Musketeers of Pig Alley* contained early versions of the gangster and victim types that have since become so familiar and Biograph's publicity

Oskar Messter

The reputation of Oskar Messter (1866–1943) has remained small because until recently early German cinema attracted little attention. Like Russia, it was considered 'backward' before about 1920. But the bare facts of Messter's career show it was highly—if unusually—developed.

As the son of an optical manufacturer, Messter was well placed to make an early technical contribution to the design of cameras and projectors. By 1897 he was selling these and offering a substantial catalogue of eighty-four films for sale.

A novel feature of Germany was the wide success of Tonbilder, with performers miming to phonograph recordings. Although Edison and Gaumont had tried to popularise these, it was Messter who succeeded in creating a large German market from 1903–13, distributing himself some 500 of the 1,500 titles in circulation. Music remained important in German cinema and Messter produced a lavish *Richard Wagner* (1912) and *Hungarian Rhapsody* (1913), both with special orchestral scores, as well as films of famous conductors in action.

His musical connections also brought him the daughter of an opera singer, Henny Porten, who became Germany's leading homegrown star after 1910, alongside the exotic Asta Nielsen. Faced with Pathé's growing dominance of the German market, stars and longer 'monopoly' films became vital to stay in business. Messter invested heavily between 1911–14. As Berlin became the centre of Germany's growing industry, he built a new studio. But the war paved the way for a government-led consolidation, the Universum Film AG or UFA, in 1917 which absorbed Messter-Film. One of his last productions was Lubitsch's breakthrough film, *Anna Boleyn*, in 1920.

Louis Feuillade

The 'French Griffith', as one historian called Louis Feuillade (1873–1925), entered the cinema in 1905, having been a cavalry officer and a journalist from 1896–1904. He joined Gaumont as head writer, working under Alice Guy, then succeeded her as the company's artistic director in 1907. This involved directing personally, supervising half-a-dozen other directors and supplying scenarios for almost everything. As a result, Feuillade has been credited with some 800 films in a career of under twenty years.

Typical examples of his early work are *The Tic* and *A Really Beautiful Woman* (both 1908), clearly improvised comedies shot on the streets of Paris. In the former, a provincial couple on their honeymoon attract a motley male following when the wife's involuntary tic is interpreted as an encouraging wink, while the latter simply records heads turning everywhere as a beautiful women passes by.

Gaumont needed distinctive product to counter Pathé's dominance and Feuillade proved versatile. He started with the 'Aesthetic Film' series of 1910, which included *Mater Dolorosa*, *Belshazzar's Feast* and *The Seven Deadly Sins*. Next came 'Life as It Is', a series of realistic social dramas, launched with *The Vipers* (1911). Nor was comedy forgotten, with over seventy episodes of the 'Baby' series from 1910–13.

But Feuillade's continuing reputation rests almost entirely on the five *Fantômas* crime series which he made in 1913-14, followed by the serials *The Vampires* (1915), *Judex* (1916), *Tih Minh* (1918) and many others. Despite the Surrealists' admiration, Feuillade was considered old-fashioned at the time of his early death, only to be rediscovered by the New Wave generation of the 1950s.

stressed that it 'showed vividly the doings of the gangster type of people'. Indeed, the future 'Lucky' Luciano was living nearby at the time and could have been among the kids who watched one of the first gangster movies being filmed. Griffith soon left New York, inspired by seeing the latest Italian spectacle, *Quo Vadis?* and determined to work on the same scale. The result would be the first American epic, *The Birth of a Nation* (1915). But there were plenty of others ready to take his place on the city streets.

The following year saw another landmark, though one that was forgotten until recently, in the broadly realistic portrayal of urban crime and vice. This was George Tucker's independent production *Traffic in Souls*, a film which boldly aimed to capitalise on public alarm over what was known as the 'white slave traffic'. White slavery, so-called, was organised prostitution which relied on women immigrants who could be intercepted as they arrived in the United States and forced to work as prostitutes, even though this was specifically outlawed by the White Slave Traffic [Mann] Act of 1910.

Tucker's film stands at the start of the documentary exposé tradition: we see newly-arrived girls being lured into prostitution; and we soon discover that the controller of the whole operation is none other than a leading moral crusader, in fact the head of the International Purity and Reform League!

Not for the last time in American cinema, a public figure is shown to be a hypocrite; and, as in the earliest crime films, there's also a fascination with the technique of both crime and its detection. Like any modern businessman, the evil William Trubus collects financial information from his brothels with up-to-date electrical gadgets, until he is eventually foiled by the sister of one of his victims and her policeman sweetheart, who eavesdrop and record their evidence on a phonograph—a prime case of the new technology and the Protestant work ethic going hand in hand.

But there was another dimension of the criminal city—the emergence of the detective as a modern hero, the only adequate guide to the city's mysteries. Although the creator of the first popular detective stories was the American Edgar Allan Poe, his example would be followed first and most enthusiastically in Europe. Baudelaire was one of his first distinguished admirers and in the story he translated, 'The Murder of Marie Roget', Poe's detective hero, Dupin, solved the murder mystery without even leaving his room, using only newspaper reports and other available evidence. Soon he was followed by Conan Doyle's Sherlock Holmes and countless other sleuths in search of ever more ingenious villains.

How this new genre reached the screen took intriguingly different forms in Europe and the United States. In Europe, and especially in France, the romantic tradition of Alexandre Dumas and Victor Hugo inspired a vast undergrowth of popular fiction which traded on the 'city mystery'—the idea of a labyrinth which is as much social and moral as physical, and can be penetrated only by the intrepid criminal mastermind and his counterpart, the equally intrepid detective (both of these usually based on British or American models).

The French company Eclair, in an effort to compete with the giants Pathé and Gaumont, launched a series of films based on the detective 'Nick Winter' in 1908. Their success led to a demand for sequels and the idea of the 'serial' was born. Eclair's Zigomar was one of the first of the catsuited master-villains. In *Zigomar Eelskin* (1913) we first meet him as an apparent corpse in a hospital mortuary, where he is about to be the subject of an autopsy. As a doctor prepares to remove some of his skin for a souvenir, his loyal female accomplice intervenes in the nick of time to spring the first of many daring escapes. The sensationalism of Zigomar and his rivals was irresistible. Pathé and Gaumont rushed to follow this innovation and, as already established international companies, their serials soon reached a global audience.

The protagonists of the 'city mystery' serial—the heroic duo of super-criminal and sleuth, both masters of

The poster for *Fantômas* (Feuillade, 1913–14) later used as a source by Magritte

disguise and escape—could be seen as extremes of 'normal' city behaviour. They operated in a heightened world of abrupt contrasts (anything can lie on the other side of a door), total illusion (nothing is what it seems), and instant transport and communication (the video phone was an early serial gadget). In these breathless tales, process takes precedence over plot; sensation over morality and paranoia over reality.

Of all the serials from the years immediately before the Great War, the one that left the most lasting impression was Louis Feuillade's *Fantômas*, based on a series of popular novels and released during 1913–14. In this, the forces of law and order are reduced to impotence, and the shadowy master-criminal with his black-clad gang prove capable of any exploit. They can steal almost invisibly, anaesthetise their victims, escape by an amazing variety of means, and their mastery of disguise makes them virtually untraceable.

A decade later, the Surrealists would celebrate the serials as the source of true poetry in cinema, for their unique combination of fantasy and realist settings. André Breton found in them 'a real sense of our century'. And the Surrealist painter René Magritte would use the image of Fantômas from the film's poster to create a brooding, nightmare figure, casting his shadow over the city, in his 1943 painting *Backfire*. This is a new and sinister development from Jules Verne's megalomaniac Captain Nemo: Fantômas isn't no one, he's everyone—or as the opening lines of Souvestre and Allain's very first story had it:

—Fantômas.
—What does that mean?
—Nothing ... and everything!
—But what is it?
—It's no one ... and yet maybe someone!
—And what does this someone do?
—He creates fear!!!

By 1915, American-made serials were beginning to dominate the market on both sides of the Atlantic. What we find in these, intriguingly, is a reversal of nineteenth-century melodrama's 'damsel in distress'. In the American serials, women *were* the central figures—whether Pearl White in *The Exploits of Elaine* or Ruth Roland in *Who Pays?*—and they were by no means victims, but detectives in their own right. Did this reflect, in some indirect way, the new role of women, emerging from Victorian gentility to take their place on the home front while the men of Europe were massacred in the trenches?

Meanwhile Feuillade created a distinctively modern 'belle dame sans merci' in the black-clad figure of Musidora—the prototype of Catwoman—in his serial *The Vampires* (1915). And a decade later, Fritz Lang's *Metropolis* would place another sinister female figure, the robot Maria, at the centre of this fable about anarchy and order. The contrast between European romantic pessimism and American sentimental optimism seems to hold true.

But elsewhere, different codes of conduct applied. Until recently, little was known of the Russian cinema which, before the Bolshevik Revolution, created a basis for Soviet cinema's purposeful new image. Yet domestic film production in Russia had accelerated rapidly after a slow start in 1908, and the social climate of its 'big city' films was different from that of both America and Western Europe. Russian high culture traditionally dealt in tragic themes, and this bias carried over into its new popular mass culture, leading to a marked preference for stories of misfortune, frustration and, frequently, death. Unlike American and West European audiences, Russians notoriously demanded sad endings—so imports were regularly equipped with these, while Russian productions intended for export sometimes had an alternative 'happy end'.

The short but impressive career of Evgeni Bauer, from 1913–17, is only beginning to attract the attention that it was denied during the Soviet era. Most of Bauer's intense and vastly popular melodramas dealt with the pressures of life in Russia's bustling new cities, often centring on an erotic passion which destroys not only women but men. The heroine of *A Child of the Big City* is an orphaned seamstress who becomes a fashionable courtesan and in the process betrays the idealistic admirer who first rescued her from poverty. In the final scene, Mary is dancing the night away with her fast set, while her distraught lover,

A Child of the Big City (Bauer, 1913)

Viktor, makes one last tragic effort to attract her attention. When this fails, he shoots himself and Mary steps over the body as she leaves in the dawn light.

The callousness of the image is perhaps more shocking today than it was to the Russian viewers of 1913, for this was becoming a familiar kind of story, as a contemporary review underlines:

Such stories have become familiar and appear rather ordinary and usual. Somehow one doesn't feel their horror ... here, beside us, amidst the commotion of the big city, perhaps everyday life destroys innocent, pure souls, celebrating victory over our indifference and egotism. So who will dare cast a stone at this abominable, repulsive being Mary [who] could only have become a greedy courtesan, having crushed and killed the noble person who loved her. And ... it is so painfully natural that, having come across his corpse on her way to gay Maxim's, she should see it only as a 'good omen'.

The image of the city in the films of the early 1910s was one that combined the reality of the modern metropolis with elements of the traditional lore of the city. Cinema relayed old myths and created new ones for the inhabitants of those cities—many of them immigrants and newcomers— and offered a space to help them adjust to the hectic, alluring and dangerous world they now inhabited.

Evgeni Bauer

The worldwide impact of Soviet cinema in the twenties effectively consigned pre-revolutionary Russian cinema to the scrapheap of history for sixty years, until a new spirit of historical inquiry reopened the vaults and discovered an extraordinary treasure-trove. In just eleven years between 1908 and 1918, it transpired that Russian production had scaled unsuspected heights of sophistication, as well as comedy, fantasy and hard-hitting social comment.

Of all the newly discovered film-makers, Evgeni Bauer (1865–1917) is the most impressive, despite a career that lasted only five years. Bauer came from a musical and theatrical family. He graduated from the Moscow Art College and was a cartoonist, theatre impresario and 'artistic' photographer before becoming a noted theatre designer.

He entered cinema as a designer on the special film produced in 1912 to mark the Tercentenary of the Romanov dynasty, then worked briefly as a director for Russian Pathé before joining Khanzhonkov's company at the end of 1913. He was soon renowned and highly paid for his spaciously designed, slow-paced and subtly-lit melodramas, many of which he scripted and often photographed as well.

These featured the most popular of the Russian stars—Vera Kholodnaya, Vera Karalli and his wife Lina Bauer—in stories of an often disturbing intensity. Sadism, self-sacrifice and madness all recur in Bauer's work, though not to the exclusion of a sly humour and passionate social conscience. Bauer died after an accident while filming in the Crimea in 1917—with one of the founders of Soviet cinema, Lev Kuleshov, as his art director. Twenty-six of the 82 films he is known to have directed survive.

3 *The Body Electric*

Thomas Edison had a new machine, the Kinetoscope, ready to sell in the spring of 1894. What he needed to convince purchasers of this peepshow was subjects that would attract the public. The obvious source was the stage, and among many vaudeville acts filmed that summer at the small black box, nicknamed the 'Black Maria', which served as his New Jersey studio, was young Annabelle Moore performing her 'Butterfly Dance'. The resulting film strip was then hand-coloured, frame by frame, to reproduce the lighting effects that Annabelle used in her stage act.

Two years after *Annabelle Dancing* was first distributed to the Edison Kinetoscope Parlours, Miss Moore herself hit the headlines and became, in a way, the first movie star. The rumour was that she had danced at a luxurious New York stag party, given by the grandson of America's leading showman, Phineas T. Barnum.

The police had been tipped off that there was more than *glace surprise* on the menu, so they raided the restaurant. Press reports claimed that Annabelle had been *asked* to appear and dance naked, but had refused. No matter: the price of copies of her film shot up from $10 to $40. She never appeared in another film, but she remained a star—even a caution for speeding down Broadway on her bicycle in 1897 made the front page of the newspapers. To be on film was to be desirable, and famous, in an unusual new way.

Sex-appeal had more to do with the invention of cinema than has usually been admitted. Conventional history suggests that the moving picture pioneers were engineers and scientists, whose invention was hijacked by unscrupulous profiteers happy to 'give the public what it wanted'. But the reality was rather different. Cinema had no single inventor. It was the invention of an era. A collective progress towards something which turned out quite differently from most expectations. A monster, which we might call 'the Modern Prometheus'—to borrow the subtitle of Mary Shelley's novel *Frankenstein*, published seventy-five years before the first pictures came to life in a New Jersey laboratory.

In practice, the development of moving pictures was immensely complex; full of reverses, blind-alleys, the blatant stealing of ideas, claims that could not be proved, and misguided obsessions. But in principle it was an amazingly clear, even simple

Left:
Annabelle Moore's rival Carmencita in a Kinetoscope loop of 1894

Below:
The first Edison Kinetoscope Parlour at 1155 Broadway, New York City

process. The desire to record and replay the human image was everywhere in the nineteenth century. It seemed—and turned out to be—only a matter of time before it became possible. And what motivated it was essentially an erotic drive.

Mary Shelley's subtitle referred to the Greek myth of the god who created human life, but was then punished for giving it the further gift of fire. If we think of fire as symbolic of desire, this is indeed at the root of what goes wrong with Victor Frankenstein's experiment. His monster is at first benign, until frustrated desire finally goads him to turn on the maker who has neglected to make him a mate.

Could science satisfy such desires? This is the question that becomes an obsession in two strange tales published within a year of each other in the early 1890s. Villiers de l'Isle Adam's *The Future Eve* and Jules Verne's *The Carpathian Castle* both involve the creation, or re-creation, through technology of an idealised woman to satisfy a man's desire. Villiers' 'android' (he coined the term we now take for granted in science fiction) is named Hadaly, after the Arabic for 'Ideal', and is made to satisfy a love-sick friend by none other than—Thomas Edison. Villiers was no Verne-like enthusiast for science and progress. Quite the contrary, he hated the trappings of modernity. But he saw in the inventor of the Phonograph potent material for a modern myth. This is how he introduced his Edison:

Here dwells Thomas Alva Edison, the man who has taken Echo captive ... his face, when studied in relation to old prints, is the image of Archimedes, of the Syracusan medallion ... Alone, seated in his American armchair, a Havana cigar between his lips—the tobacco transforming his virile projects into reveries— staring distractedly ahead, wrapped in his already legendary garment of purple-tasseled black silk, he appeared lost in the depths of meditation.

The real Edison was indeed popularly known as 'the wizard of Menlo Park' (after the site of his first laboratory) and happy to be thought responsible for almost every modern invention. But what Villiers attributed to him in his novel was closer to the perverse world of the French 'Decadents'. It was the creation of a woman 'less artificial' than modern women seemed to reactionaries like Villiers, a kind of purified essence. 'Edison' explains to his client that Hadaly has been brought to life by electricity—'this spark, bequeathed by Prometheus'—and programmed with

seven hours of speech ... composed by our greatest poets, our subtlest metaphysicians, the deepest novelists of our century upon my commission ... And never will Hadaly's speech deceive your expectations ... With her you need never—as with the live model—fear misunderstanding.

Thomas Edison

The more we know about Thomas Alva Edison (1847–1931), the harder it is to relate his 1895 vision of an audiovisual library for the future to a relentless twenty-year legal battle over an invention in which he took little direct interest. Yet it was the appeal and saleability of his Phonograph and Kinetoscope which pointed the way towards a commercial film industry, even if neither provided a useful model for its technical development.

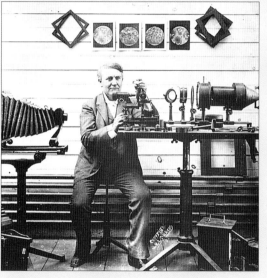

Edison was already a myth in his own time, with a lack of formal education and his early enterprise casting him in the Benjamin Franklin mould of homespun American genius. But above all it was his identification with electricity—as inventor of the light bulb and pioneer of electrical distribution—which gave him mythic status as arch-creator of the future.

It was his dogged pursuit of sound recording in the late 1870s that paved the way for an equally determined attack on image recording in the late eighties, apparently inspired by Muybridge's Zoopraxiscope. Working under his direction between 1889–93, Dickson, Brown and Lauste created the Kinetoscope viewer, the Kinetograph camera and the 'Black Maria' studio.

When it became clear that projection rather than peep-show was the public's preferred means of viewing, Edison bought Armat's projector and on 23 April 1896 publicly launched this as the Edison Vitascope, showing Kinetoscope loops and a Robert Paul film.

While his own film sales languished through lack of investment, Edison poured resources into suing other movie entrepreneurs. From 1909 his Motion Picture Patents Company (known as the 'Trust') successfully intimidated independents, until a 1915 anti-trust ruling ended its power. In 1918, Edison closed his Bronx studio and left the business he had both created and hampered.

J. Stuart Blackton

James Blackton packed half a dozen careers into thirty years as a pioneering film-maker. Born in Sheffield in 1875, he was taken to the US ten years later. His first job was as a newspaper illustrator. He also practised 'lightning sketches' as a vaudeville act. A meeting with Edison in 1896 led to his appearance in early Kinetoscope films drawing before the camera.

Blackton was intrigued, and in 1897 bought an Edison projector which he converted to a camera. The Vitagraph Company which he founded with two partners began making topical films about the Spanish–American War and news stories in New York. Blackton also starred in their 'Happy Hooligan' series. The studio which Vitagraph built in 1903 in Flatbush was considered the most modern of its time, and soon Blackton was directing more ambitious films there, such as *A Gentleman of France* and *Raffles, the Amateur Cracksman*.

Blackton pioneered drawn and object animation. His *Humorous Phases of Funny Faces* (1906) used a lightning sketch technique for a comic narrative, while the influential *Haunted Hotel* (1906) moved objects around the bemused hero by means of single frame exposure.

In 1908, Blackton started a realist drama series, 'Scenes of True Life', which had an impact in many countries, and took Vitagraph upmarket by filming Shakespeare and the classics. He was, however, soon forced to delegate responsibility to others. During the Great War he produced propaganda films and in 1920 moved to England, where he made historical dramas, including two in colour. After losing everything in the 1929 Wall Street crash, Blackton returned to the US, where he worked as a production supervisor until his death in 1941.

In Jules Verne's *The Carpathian Castle*, a beautiful singer dies in mid-performance leaving two of her admirers heartbroken. Years later, while travelling in the remote Carpathians, one of them hears her voice and, after breaking into a castle which turns out to belong to his former rival, discovers the diva once again performing. But as he rushes to rescue her, it cruelly transpires that her image is only projected and her voice a recording!

Villiers' and Verne's novels appeared in 1891 and 1892, a year before Edison and Dickson publicly launched the Kinetoscope. There is no way that either of these very different characters could have had any direct knowledge of the experiments under way in New Jersey. But both were sensitive to a 'life wish' that was common in the late nineteenth century. Indeed Edison might almost have been quoting Verne when he foresaw in 1895 the union of the phonograph and moving pictures enabling 'grand opera to be given at the Metropolitan Opera House in New York ... with artists and musicians long since dead'.

The one pioneer of moving pictures whom both Villiers and Verne could have known about—and almost certainly did—was Eadweard Muybridge. This eccentric English photographer, who played almost no part in developing either the technology or the 'ideology' of cinema none the less served as a vital catalyst of what was to come. Like his contemporary the French scientist Etienne-Jules Marey, who was equally remote from any concept of cinema, Muybridge offered a quasi-scientific spectacle which was close enough to Victorian obsessions to attract a wide following. Innocently, these two helped prepare their generation for the motion picture era.

The known facts of Muybridge's life sound more like a Western novel than a Victorian scientific biography. Baptised Edward Muggeridge in 1830 at Kingston upon Thames, he set off as a young man to seek his fortune on the west coast of the United States. By the mid-1850s he was established in the book trade in San Francisco, but then suffered serious injuries in a stagecoach accident. Back in England recuperating, he studied the new art of photography and returned to America in 1866 as a landscape photographer. His studies of California, Alaska and Central America culminated in a photographic panorama of San Francisco. Eadweard Muybridge (as he now called himself) had become a specialist in the monumental stillness that early photography unavoidably conferred on its subjects, with its need for long exposures.

1889 illustration of Muybridge lecturing

Fate intervened again in the shape of a former Governor of California with a passion for horses. Leland Stanford thought that trotting and galloping horses did not move as artists had traditionally shown them. He believed that they had all four hooves off the ground at some point in their gait. And this he now wanted a photographer to prove—according to legend it was to settle a bet, which presumably made a good story then, as now. The first results in 1872 were primitive, but apparently sufficient to encourage Leland to continue funding Muybridge's elaborate experiments at Palo Alto.

Meanwhile, Muybridge's life took another melodramatic turn. He discovered that the son his wife had recently borne was another man's, so he set out to find and shoot the suspected lover. Six months later he was acquitted of murder and able to resume both landscape photography and eventually his analysis of motion under Stanford's patronage.

Plate from Muybridge's Pennsylvania period, 'Woman with a parasol'

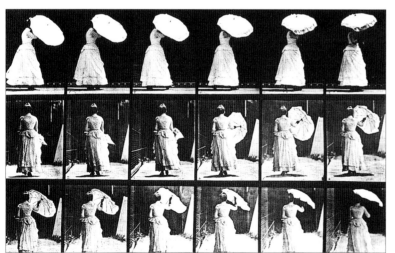

The sequences of frozen movement that Muybridge produced, with the technical help of a railway engineer to design his apparatus, were widely reproduced around the world. Today they look like so many frames from a filmstrip, but at the time they were hailed as proof of photography's ability to halt time and motion and put these under scrutiny.

However the rich optical culture of the nineteenth century soon suggested that these images could be re-animated, in the way that Thaumatropes and Zoetropes had already entertained several generations with an illusion of movement based on the eye's capacity to 'fuse' adjacent images. Essentially Muybridge combined the rotating disc of the Zoetrope with the Magic Lantern in a device he called the Zoopraxiscope. Armed with this and his growing repertoire of 'animal locomotion' studies, he started a new career as a popular lecturer in 1880. A California newspaper wrote prophetically:

Mr Muybridge has laid the foundation of a new method of entertaining the people, and we predict that his instantaneous, photographic, magic lantern zoetrope will make the rounds of the civilised world.

Muybridge did make the rounds of the civilised world over the next fifteen years, and his acclaimed lecture-demonstrations—members of the British royal family and the poet laureate Alfred Tennyson attended one in 1882—effectively created an enthusiasm for the spectacle of moving photography before there existed any other means to satisfy it.

By the mid-1880s Muybridge had fallen out with Stanford and was installed at the university in Philadelphia, partly on the initiative of the painter Thomas Eakins. There he proceeded to create a bizarre world of animals and, increasingly, semi-clothed and naked human figures—all photographed in front of the squared grid that that gave his work an aura of scientific rigour. What seems obvious today, although it may not have in the strange climate of Victorian self-delusion over sexuality, is that Muybridge was creating a new kind of erotic display.

Many of his tableaux seem to hover between two worlds: the languorous, undraped ancient Mediterranean world imagined by salon painters like Sir Lawrence Alma-Tadema, and the new sciences of physiology, anthropology and work study. They cast a cold, photographic eye on miniature dramas which attract and titillate us: clothes being removed, water poured over bodies, naked figures engaged in strange rituals. Others show grotesquely mishapen figures, amputees and the obese, in scenes which recall the Victorian popularity of the fairground freak show. In doing so, they secrete a powerful new voyeuristic appeal—which Muybridge must have known and felt. Indeed, his notebook entries indicate that he did. What was published as 'One Woman Disrobing Another' he called 'Inspecting a Slave (White)'; while 'Turning around in Surprise and Running Away' is described in his notebook more suggestively as 'Ashamed'.

The sheer scale and eccentricity of Muybridge's work, running as it did to many thousands of photo-sequences, invites speculation. Why did he not experiment further with projection techniques, preferring instead to publish his work in books? How much did he in fact contribute to the major achievements usually credited to him? Did he really understand the implications of his work? Hollis Frampton suggested a daring hypothesis which tries to answer at least some of these questions. After the trauma of shooting his wife's lover, followed by imprisonment and a dramatic trial, might Muybridge have become unconsciously fixated on 'the decisive moment' and sought to relive it endlessly in his zoetrope sequences? In other words, was Muybridge the first to discover the fascination of the 'action replay' as an intrinsic part of cinema's appeal?

Coincidentally, Muybridge and Marey were born in the same year, 1830, and both died in 1904. The symmetry and links between their lives are intriguing. Stanford was apparently first drawn to the scientific study of equestrian movement by discovering Marey's 1873 book, *Animal Mechanism*. Marey was then inspired to use photography by reading about Muybridge's work and welcomed him to Paris in 1881—where the latter probably learned how to improve his projection system, which in turn seems to have inspired Edison.

It is traditional to say that Marey remained a scientist while Muybridge was more of a dilettante. But Marey's own multiple exposure 'chrono-photographs' of black-and-white-suited gymnasts have an even more modern poetry than Muybridge's tableaux. They represent the very image of 'time transfixed' in dense, mysterious images which were to influence Cubist and Surrealist painting, and also find an echo in the fantasy underworld of serials like Feuillade's *Fantômas* and *The Vampires*.

At the height of his fame, in 1888, Muybridge demonstrated his Zoopraxiscope to Edison and the latter wrote in his notebook that he was now experimenting with an instrument that would 'do for the Eye what the phonograph did for the Ear'. The work took four years of intermittent effort, with Edison's Scottish assistant William Dickson playing the most active part. And when the apparatus was ready to demonstrate, it is striking that the first test films looked remarkably like Muybridge's 'studies'. A handshake (between Dickson and another employee), a boxing bout, fencing and a blacksmith scene—these were all shot during 1892–3 against a black background, with the action directly addressed to the camera.

They are also exclusively male scenes, which is hardly surprising since the performers were all Edison employees. But once the Kinetoscope was launched commercially, something more enticing would be needed. There was already an indication of this at the time of the famous *Record of a Sneeze*, often misleadingly described as Edison's first film. This came about when a reporter from *Harper's Weekly* wrote to Edison suggesting that he 'have some nice looking young person perform a sneeze for the Kinetograph'. To ensure coverage of his new invention in the magazine, Edison complied—but the sneeze was 'performed', not by the girl clearly intended by *Harper's*, but by a middle-aged mustachioed employee, Fred Ott. Only after the first New York Kinetoscope Parlour opened in April 1894, did audience demand have to be taken more seriously. Soon Annabelle and her rival Carmencita were invited to the Black Maria to perform their already acclaimed stage routines for this novel 'electric vaudeville'.

But something had changed, and would change again when Edison was forced by competition to abandon the peep-show form and take to the big

One of the special suits worn for Marey's 'chronophotographs', and the results obtained

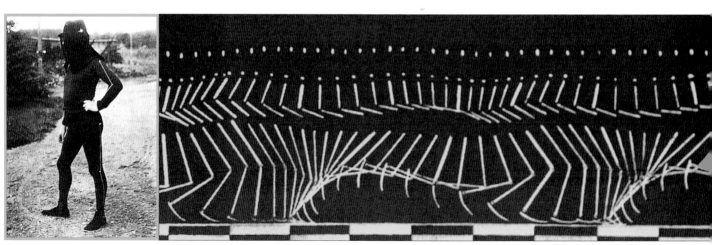

screen. For the solitary viewer's experience of the Kinetoscope is very much like spying on something clandestinely. In a theatre, with the same image projected on a screen, the effect is rather different. Surrounded by other viewers, probably strangers and of both sexes, watching someone who is oblivious of being watched could be distinctly embarrassing. As if in recognition of this, an early Kinetoscope loop of a belly dancer, Fatima, was apparently 'censored' with a heavy pattern of bars when it was to be transferred to the screen. However, in this early case the censorship was more symbolic than efficient, since the bars obscure almost everything *except* Fatima's unclothed belly.

One way to 'frame' the new moving pictures was to include a proxy viewer in the picture. And if the subject was one likely to cause embarrassment, then the substitute viewer could take the blame. How else to explain the little dramas of punishment or frustration that are acted out in so many very early films, as Peeping Toms hiding behind screens and using telescopes are discovered by their indignant victims? This denouement saves face for all concerned by disrupting what would otherwise be an 'impossible' final disclosure—and sometimes providing its own compensatory pleasures. In Bitzer's *Peeping Tom in the Dressing Room* (Biograph, 1905) a theatre voyeur is discovered and teasingly punished by the chorus girls who are the object of his attention and who then beat him with powder puffs.

The 'keyhole' version of this basic scenario also proved useful as a way of structuring longer and more varied films. In Fitzhamon's *The Inquisitive Boots* (Hepworth, 1905), a prying hotel boots leads us from door to door as he returns polished shoes. In each case, he mimes some hint of what lies within, before we see it through a keyhole-shaped mask. Expectations are raised by seeing a woman writing a love letter in the first room, but the film ends after several anodyne revelations with the boots being

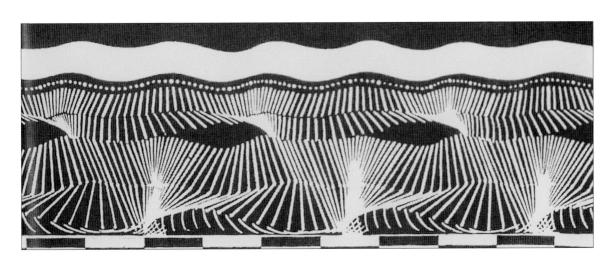

'justified' when a snooping concierge discovers a room on fire and is able to call the fire brigade.

Pointing the camera literally through a keyhole cut-out probably seemed rather crude, even by 1903. There were already subtler ways of controlling the extraordinary sexual power of the new medium. In Porter's *The Gay Shoe Clerk* (Biograph, 1903), as noted earlier, the younger of two women boldly encourages a salesman by raising her skirt while he attends to her shoes. The fact that we follow this mutual seduction in an inserted close-up has the effect of blanking out embarrassment, disbelief, disapproval and any other emotions this surprisingly direct little film may originally have aroused. As erotic tension rises with the girl's skirt, our attention is held on the tantalising calf—until the clerk lunges forward to kiss her and, now back in a wider shot, 'reality' crashes in with the girl's chaperone indignantly attacking the clerk and bringing the film to an end.

Until around 1906 the range of material supplied by many reputable commercial companies included films that were certainly considered immoral by a large proportion of the audience—

squirted in the face through a keyhole by an indignant guest. Biograph's *A Search for the Evidence* (1903), unusually, follows a woman searching a rooming house by the same means. Finally, she and her male companion (the owner or a detective?) find their quarry; at which point our viewpoint changes to inside the room where the erring husband is *in flagrante* with another woman. Another variation occurs in Pathé's *Scenes at Every Floor* (1904), where voyeurism is

while also being much in demand by others. An anecdote from the early days of Kinetoscope parlours reveals the dilemma this posed. This is from a letter received by an operator in Butte, Montana, from his distributor:

We are confident that the Dolorita *Passion Dance* would be as exciting as you desire. In fact, we will not show it in our parlour. You speak of the class of trade which wants something of this character ... A man in Buffalo has one of these films and informs us that he frequently has forty or fifty men waiting in line to see it.

France had an established reputation as the main source of risqué material in all forms—so much so that the mere use of a French word or a reference to 'Parisian' was enough to signal titillation. Photography had already created a vast market in visual eroticism during the second half of the nineteenth century, starting with daguerreotypes of classically posed nudes and soon branching out into much more explicit scenes of seduction. A 1903 American film entitled *Art Studies* need only show two men leafing through a magazine with leering grimaces to evoke the excitement these images caused in a puritanical society.

The stereoscope, allowing individual viewers to see images with a striking illusion of realistic depth, proved especially suited to pornographic purposes. 'Artistic' poses, based on the same classical themes that had long served painters, were now joined by scenes more obviously set in brothels, catering for specialised tastes among their male clientele. These images remained largely the preserve of the wealthy and sophisticated, until a sudden craze for picture postcards swept them into the mass market. Although the picture postcard was initially a German enthusiasm, it was boosted by the Paris Universal Exposition of 1889 which also saw the Eiffel Tower built and Thomas Edison hailed as the wizard of electricity. Sending a card from the top of the Eiffel Tower was a hugely popular pastime which helped link tourism and postcards. But soon there were also cards definitely not intended for sending to family and friends.

These 'French cards' took increasing advantage of cheap photographic reproduction techniques after 1900, and became an important business for the hawkers and traders in the Paris arcades. The traditional subjects they used as a pretext for female nudity (and male lechery)—ancient Rome, slave markets, the sultan's harem—were the same that early film-makers would soon bring to life, albeit more chastely. But equally often their seductions and

A typical stereoscopic 'artistic subject' from 1887

stripteases were set in a fictionalised present, the romantically licentious Paris of the Belle Epoque.

French film producers were not slow to see the potential of bringing these embryonic narratives to the screen. A Pathé production of 1905, entitled *Transparent Cards*, is typical of what the sales catalogues already classified as 'bawdy scenes of a piquant nature'. Interestingly, it uses another by-product of the new industrialised eroticism as a dramatic device: a young man finds a set of risqué playing cards hidden at the bottom of a cigar box and when he starts to look at them they 'come to life', with each one showing successive stages of a model's striptease. As such films began circulating widely, opposition began to mount. In France, it was led by the Catholic Church, with a ringing denunciation in 1906 of all such 'immodest' films, postcards and illustrated papers. In America, as already noted, the nickelodeons were threatened with summary closure for 'immorality' in 1908.

As censorship, both voluntary and involuntary, came into force everywhere in the last years of the decade, overtly erotic films went underground—becoming in the process more narrowly pornographic. Known as 'smokers' or 'stag movies' in the United States, after the all-male occasions when they were shown, these were also shown 'after hours' in many big-city cinemas, and reputedly became a feature of European brothels. Mainstream commercial cinema was now keen to stress its respectability. But even as it set out to recapture the middle-class and especially the female audience, this audience was itself changing. Cinema would now play

Poster for a 1909 Max Linder film

an active part in this process—offering, quite literally, new images of men, women and their relationships.

One sign of the times was the appearance of a French actor who quickly set a new style in screen comedy. Max Linder was quite openly a ladies' man. He pursued women on screen with energy and wit, and women in the audience clearly enjoyed watching him do so. Max, as he soon became known, was one of the first—if not the first—true international film stars. Before him there had been plenty of energetic

Max Linder

Although Max Linder (1882–1925) was the most inventive and influential of early screen comedians, he was not the first. The idea of a stock character in an endless series of film sketches had already been launched by Pathé's 'André Deed', as the first of their many assembly-line comics.

Linder was born Gabriel-Maximilien Leuvielle in the Gironde, and appeared on the provincial stage before reaching Paris in 1904, where he found work at a theatre which had close links with Pathé. He started playing minor film parts and continued to act on stage—until, in 1907, one of Pathé's comedy stars left and vacated the character of an elegant young dandy. This Linder adopted, and his aptly titled *A Skater's Debut* appeared in December to wide acclaim.

'Max' was soon turning out a film a week, directed at first by Gasnier, then by Zecca, Nonguet and other

Pathé regulars, until in 1910 he took over himself. Between 1907 and 1914, he made some 360 comedies for Pathé and became a world celebrity.

The mainspring of Linder's comedy was sexual attraction. Always ready for an amorous adventure, Max becomes embroiled in fantastic ruses and impersonations to avoid punishment. Though invariably elegant and sophisticated, he is often incompetent and deluded—dreams and drunkenness were regular excuses for fantasy.

In 1916, Linder went to the US to work for Essanay (which had just lost Chaplin, who acknowledged Linder's influence), but neither this nor a second American spell in 1921 proved successful. Linder never fully recovered from being gassed early in the First World War. He died in 1925 in a suicide pact with his young wife.

Alice Guy

The 'world's first woman director' was probably also its first fiction director when she took charge of making the films urgently needed to stimulate her employer's equipment sales. Alice Guy (1873–1968) joined the Gaumont company as a secretary in 1896 but soon found herself making *The Fairy of the Cabbages* in Léon Gaumont's garden beside his factory.

For the next ten years, 'Mademoiselle Alice' supervised all Gaumont's production and personally directed much of it. Among the films attributed to her are *Madame Has Cravings* (1906), in which a pregnant

woman voraciously helps herself to absinthe and a pipe with disastrous results, and *On the Barricade* (1907), about a mother and son caught up in a street battle. Her *Life of Christ* (1906, co-directed with Jasset) was one of the most impressive in this popular genre.

Guy was also responsible for Gaumont's musical 'phonoscènes' and footage exists of her directing one of these (probably a scene from the opera *Mignon*) with a large cast and extensive lighting and sound playback equipment.

In 1907, Guy married a former Gaumont cameraman, Herbert Blaché, and they left for the US to establish a small Gaumont studio in Cleveland. But Gaumont's American venture did not prosper, and in 1910 the Guy-Blachés established an independent company, Solax, first in New York and later at Fort Lee, New Jersey. Few of her many American films survive, but they had a reputation for quality. However, Guy left independent production in 1917 to direct for Pathé-Exchange and Metro, but when her marriage broke up in 1922 she returned to France, never again to work as a film-maker.

Both sides of
the fence in
Women's Rights
(Bamforth, 1900)

clowning; and at least one successful international screen comedian, André Deed (known disconcertingly as 'Cretinetti' in his Italian films, and as 'Boireau' in France). But Max was handsome, always elegant and a sophisticated man about town. He was someone to admire—maybe even fall in love with.

Linder mixed elegance with absurdity. His physical routines, though improvised on a tight production schedule, were endlessly inventive and beautifully executed. His adventures in pursuit of pretty *Parisiennes* allowed the male figure to become consciously attractive. The films become like an extended courtship dance, addressed to an increasingly sophisticated audience with all the efficiency of Pathé's international distribution.

He had started on the stage, playing everything from vaudeville to classics, but soon realised that screen technique was different. It was necessary to be subtle, he believed, and slapstick had to be sudden and unexpected to work on film. In fact, as he explained in 1916, the screen comedian has to 'think more' than his stage equivalent.

Mack Sennett learned from Linder that screen chases have to be carefully plotted. Chaplin referred to him as 'the master'. And Sennett and Chaplin weren't the only film comedians to learn from Linder: Buster Keaton, Harold Lloyd, and Laurel and Hardy all took something from his pioneering example. They discovered the importance of poise and dignity among the pratfalls, and how to create a true screen character—although the characters they created proved better suited to the American melting pot than Max's debonair Paris playboy.

Women also were beginning to look different on and off the screen. As the new century dawned, dress was a controversial issue, foreshadowing the bitter struggles of the suffragists and birth-control campaigners. The *Daily Mail* noted in 1900 that one of the most remarkable products of the later nineteenth century had been 'the athletic young woman, the Amazon of the mountains, the moors and the playing fields'.

It was the bicycle that had first liberated women, and one early British film showed precisely what had first alarmed traditionalists about women cycling. George Smith's *As Seen Through a Telescope* (1900) has a man spying on a woman's ankle as she prepares to mount a bicycle. Soon even the secrets of the gymnasium were on public display in a series of American films clearly built around the appeal to both sexes of *The Physical Culture Girl* (Biograph, 1903). *The Physical Culture Lesson* (1906) went so far as to show a man leading a woman through exercises before pulling her on to his lap for a passionate embrace. And in the slightly surreal *Athletic Girl and the Burglar* (Biograph, 1905), a woman breaks off her exercise routines to knock insensible a passing burglar.

Production photograph from Paul Poiret's 1910 fashion film

If these suggest a tongue-in-cheek attitude to women's new-found independence, the contrast with censorious British attitudes is instructive. One British film has long been known to cinema historians as *Ladies Skirts Nailed to a Fence* (Bamforth, 1900), a primitive example of joining two shots together to show front and rear views of a scene. Little attention has been paid to motivation or context, since the point of the film was assumed to be the prank of two mischievous youths nailing the women's skirts to the fence while they talk.

However, the recent discovery of an original catalogue which lists the film as *Women's Rights* and a spoken text intended to accompany it, reveals this to be a malicious satire on women's new militancy:

'As if we downtrod women hadn't any common rights.'
Stood Mr Niggle listening to all they had to say.
'We'll get their tails in quietly and nail them to the boards.'
They fished for and their tails they hooked without the slightest noise.
While Niggle and his worthy boy in flight now safety seeks.
And now behold the champions of women's every right.

Thirteen years later, after a decade of rising violence on the part of suffragists demanding the vote for women, another British comedy illuminated popular attitudes towards this struggle. *Milling the Militants* (Percy Stow, 1913) shows a disgruntled husband dreaming while his wife is taking part in a suffrage demonstration. Imagining himself Prime Minister, he first decrees that she and her comrades will wear men's clothing and be forced to do road repairs in a chain gang. He then orders his wife to be ducked in the pond in a parody of the classic witchcraft 'test'. The film may be subtitled *A Comical Absurdity*, but in the same year that saw Emily Davidson's protest suicide at the Derby—all the more shocking for being captured 'live' on film—it offers some insight into the fears that women's militancy had provoked and is all the more revealing for being cast in this fantasy form.

Women were marching and going on hunger strike (and taking care that their demonstrations were advantageously filmed). They were also experiencing another kind of liberation through, of all things, fashion. After the excesses of the crinoline, the bustle and punitive corseting to achieve an hour-glass figure, there was a radical new shape. In Paris, Paul Poiret drew his inspiration from the Grecian style of the 1790s Directoire period, and from newly fashionable Japanese and other exotic sources. He abandoned the cinched waist for designs that fell from the shoulder in elegant arabesques, Fashion, as one of his customers, the society beauty Lady Diana Cooper, said gratefully, 'had finally come round to us'. Poiret travelled widely, preaching his new doctrine of 'naturalness' and, from 1910, illustrating his lectures with specially made films—until one of these was confiscated as obscene when he travelled to the United States in 1913.

1910 was in fact when fashion first became a

This technique became common in the early years of the century on both sides of the Atlantic. It allowed lettering and cut-outs to form their own shapes (*How Jones Lost His Roll*), toys to come to life (*The Humpty Dumpty Circus, The Toymaker and the Good Fairy*), and added the supernatural to spooky comedies (*A Visit to the Spiritualist, The Mesmerist and the Country Couple*). It was not until 1906 that Blackton, now a partner in Edison's rival, the Vitagraph Company, made what was drawn the film's content in *Humorous Phases of Funny Faces*. Blackton's hand is still visible in the corner of the frame, as if to reassure viewers about how the drawings were made, but this marks the start of animation as the conjuring of a fictional world entirely by graphic means.

More impressive at the time was Blackton's next venture into 'object animation' in *The Haunted Hotel* (Vitagraph, 1907), where the contents of the hotel enjoy an eerie life of their own. The success of this film in France, as almost everywhere, encouraged Léon Gaumont to back one of his staff, the ex-illustrator and cartoonist Emile Cohl, as an animator. Cohl was to use many different animation techniques and often combine these in the same film. His *The Tenants Next Door* (1909) adapted the established comic-strip format of two adjacent rooms, which we see as two interacting worlds—here linked by yet another variation on the familiar theme of voyeurism, now given a fantastic dimension. An old couple are spying through a hole on the young lovers next door, when one of these turns out to be a magician who goes through an extraordinary gamut of transformations as he teases and punishes the voyeurs.

Cohl and the other illustrators who crossed over into animation, like Winsor McCay and the Fleishers, remained close to their roots in the world of 1890s commercial art. What they thought of such movements as Cubism and Futurism we can only infer from parodies like

A 1908 French magazine article explaining trick film effects

Cohl's *The Neo-Impressionist Painter* (1910) and his later *Futurist and Incoherent Paintings* (1916). But the same Cubists and Futurists, as eager consumers of popular entertainment, were none the less part of their audience. And it is difficult not to believe that these artists were as inspired by the playful reflexivity of Cohl's films as they had been by the bold abstraction of tribal and naive painting. Indeed Cohl's *The Mysterious Fine Arts* (1910) could plausibly be compared with the Cubists' radical questioning of illusionism, since it works through all the processes of picture-making available at the time.

Early animation often seems, with hindsight, like a popular version of the same concerns that pushed 'serious' artists into Modernism. And even if Picasso apparently decided against experimenting with film around 1912, his fellow-Cubist Léger eventually made an outstanding film, *Mechanical Ballet*, in 1924. But other currents within the cinema of this time were also distorting the human form in startling, suggestive ways.

Electricity had seemed to the late nineteenth century a magical new force, capable of anything and everything. This enthusiasm often appears as a source of comedy in early films. *A Lesson in Electricity* is typical: it starts with a teacher encouraging his class to experiment by running electric current through various subjects. In his absence, they raise the stakes by turning a stretch of pavement into a 'live' test zone, so that a string of passers-by are soon joined in a helpless 'electrified' conga.

The humour of many early films is sardonic and physically violent by modern standards. When a woman offender is held forcibly in a chair to be photographed for police records and resists by making a series of remarkable grimaces (*A Subject for the Rogues' Gallery*, also known as *Photographing a Female Crook*, Biograph 1904), we wonder if this is a performance after all. Likewise, a 'machine' which appears to convert live animals directly into sausages in *Mechanical Butchery* (Lumière, 1895) is obviously a music-hall joke, but a disturbing one. A transplanted arm which turns out to have a criminal life of its own in *The Thieving Hand* (Vitagraph 1908) and the alarming 'cures' offered by *Dr Skinum* (Biograph, 1907) are closer to pantomime, but they still play effectively on atavistic fears of the body being 'possessed'.

Most disturbing of all, from a modern perspective, is the delight that many early films take in amputation and dismemberment. This was one of Méliès' specialities. The image of his own head is blown up like a balloon until it bursts in *The Man with the India-Rubber Head* (1902), and in *The Melomaniac* (1903), he 'grows' no fewer than six successive heads. In one of Méliès' recently rediscovered films, *Turn of the Century Surgery* (1902), a patient has all his limbs first removed then replaced by a breezy surgeon. A similar routine appears in *The Good Child and the Veteran* (Gaumont, 1908), where the leader of a gang of children playing in the park approaches a military veteran and 'borrows' from him, one by one, all his limbs, and finally even his head, for their games. In

the end, they return everything and the veteran is happily reassembled.

What are we to make of this and similar fantasies of dismemberment? At one level, they are perhaps simply evidence of a more robust style of humour in an era when life was more uncertain and medicine less resourceful. But they also testify to a particular, and rather perverse, pleasure that film supplied: that of treating the living body as a machine, or a toy—something which can be taken apart and reassembled at will. It is the pleasure that children explore with dolls; and one that Walt Whitman celebrated in his great Blakean ode to sexuality, 'I sing the body electric'. We also cannot forget that so many films of fantastic dismemberment appeared on the eve of the First World War, which would brutally slaughter and maim so many of those who had been cinema's first spectators. It is almost as if the films were an unconscious collective rehearsal for the mayhem of the Western Front.

One of the poets to emerge from the War, Siegfried Sassoon, may have had this connection in mind (as well as a memory of *Omar Khayyám*) when he wrote the poem 'Picture-Show':

And still they come and go: and this is all I know—
That from the gloom I watch an endless picture-show,
Where wild or listless faces flicker on their way (...)

And still, between the shadow and the blinding flame,
The brave despair of men flings onward, ever the same
As in those doom-lit years that wait them, and have been ...
And life is just the picture dancing on a screen.

Asta Nielsen

Already an actress at the Copenhagen Royal Theatre before she started making films in 1910, Asta Nielsen (1883–1972) quickly established herself as the first truly international female star. After her debut with August Blom, she moved to Germany and had a huge success with *The Abyss*, which was directed by Urban Gad, with whom she formed a close professional and personal partnership (they were married from 1912–26). She spent the rest of her film career in Germany, although her films circulated in many countries.

Her image was that of a beautiful *femme fatale*, but with a notably fashionable and often ironic modern style. In 1913, for example, she appeared in *The Film Prima Donna* and *The Suffragette*, both highly contemporary subjects. It is perhaps easier to grasp Nielsen's impact from contemporary testimony than from surviving, often incomplete prints. She was noted for unusual restraint in an age of exaggerated acting, and also for a sense of humour rare among early film stars.

In 1920, she produced and starred in Sven Gade's *Hamlet*—not as a male impersonator, but as a princess in a Danish tale who masquerades as a prince! A series of major dramatic roles followed: *Mata Hari* (1921), *Pandora's Box* and *Earthspirit* (1922–3), *Miss Julie* (1922) and *Hedda Gabler* (1924). One of her last roles was in Pabst's *Joyless Street* (1925), together with the still unknown Garbo and Dietrich. Evidence of her enduring fame came when Goebbels offered her a studio in 1933 if she would come out of retirement in Denmark and return to Germany. She refused.

4 *Real Lives*

The Victorians felt ambivalent about reality. Being there, doing it, seeing with one's own eyes—these were all attractive for men, and women, of action. But was it not equally satisfying to visit by proxy, to travel without leaving home, to range across centuries and millennia while remaining in the present? To have the world and its history at one's fingertips was an attractive alternative to the world of action, as countless readers of Verne and Haggard testified. Books were the traditional source of this satisfaction. Now there was another.

Robert Paul was the first to tap an audience's fascination with this new experience through moving pictures. He photographed the Derby in 1896 and managed to have his film ready to show on the following evening at the Alhambra Theatre in London. With the theatre orchestra playing 'God Bless the Prince of Wales', a packed house saw Prince Edward's horse Persimmon win. The audience demanded a replay, and another, discovering the joys of remote control. Reality would never be the same again.

Five years later, the idea of filming *unstaged* history was inadvertently born amid the fake classicism of the 1901 Pan-American Exposition at Buffalo, New York. Edison had an exclusive contract to film at the expo and his cameramen were making a series of routine records of President McKinley's visit. They filmed him reviewing a guard of honour and making a speech; and they were waiting for him to emerge from the Temple of Music. Suddenly word spread among the assembled crowd: the president had been shot by an assassin inside the Temple. The

cameraman took a panorama as word of the tragedy spread, and the resulting *Mob Outside the Temple of Music* became a strangely poignant record of the tragedy.

Edison cameramen continued to film the events that followed. After McKinley died several days later, the first stage of his elaborate funeral took place at Buffalo, before continuing in Washington and finishing at his hometown in Ohio. This brought the total coverage of the Exposition and its tragic aftermath to eleven films, all of them 'actualities' until what should have been the climax of the series—the execution of the President's assassin, an anarchist named Czolgosz. When Edison's cameramen James White and Edwin Porter were refused permission to film the execution at Albany Jail, they resorted to staging it themselves, and setting the scene with a 'real' exterior of the jail.

However the film recommended to exhibitors to end their very popular 'McKinley' shows was not this part-faked *Execution of Czolgosz*. It was a wholly

Far left and left: *The Executiion of Czolgosz* (Edison, 1901) combined actuality dramatisation

manufactured item entitled *The Martyred Presidents*, which showed memorial portraits of Lincoln, Garfield and McKinley set in a monument, flanked by a mourner and the allegorical figure of Justice. The gravity of the subject had apparently triggered a traditional response from Edison's production department, for this is clearly a lantern-slide sequence realised on film. But it would not have surprised the audiences of 1901, who were still more familiar with lantern-show conventions than with those of moving pictures.

What was universally known as the Magic Lantern by the nineteenth century first appeared two centuries earlier as a development of the camera obscura used by artists to aid picture-making. With the addition of a lens and a lamp, this had become the 'lanthorn, with pictures in glasse, to make strange things appear on a wall' which Samuel Pepys bought in 1666. Lanterns continued to be used for whimsical and atmospheric entertainment on an intimate scale until the early nineteenth century, when a succession of technical developments turned the lantern show into a mainstay of Victorian life.

New sources of illumination (limelight, gas and eventually electricity) enabled projection to take place before ever larger audiences. Then photography began to extend dramatically the limited range of painted slides available. Finally multiple lanterns and mechanical slides introduced many kinds of spectacular dissolving effects. By the last decades of the century, lantern showmanship was a sophisticated audiovisual entertainment, operating in many different genres. Many of its features, such as musical accompaniment, a narrator and a mixture of items, would carry over directly into early film presentation. Indeed lantern slides and moving pictures would coexist on equal terms for over a decade after 1895, before the lantern was relegated to church halls, only to re-emerge in the guise of the modern slide projector.

One lantern show genre which started to take on a life of its own in the 1860s was the travel lecture. There were many objective reasons for this. Travel itself was becoming easier and faster, thanks to railways, steamships and canals. A growing middle class was interested in the wider world and increasingly likely to travel abroad. But the popular travel lecture was also an entertainment form in itself: it meant an escape from routine, a reverie in the dark in the company of an eloquent lecturer, exotic images and stories which could be justified as 'improving', and of course a socially acceptable occasion to meet one's friends.

In the United States, travel lecturers became popular celebrities, able to fill the largest halls and theatres and attracting audiences of several thousand to their 'courses'. The leading American lecturer of the eighties and nineties was John Stoddard, who started by using available material but soon became an active producer, commissioning his own slides on extended tours of his chosen countries. Stoddard made a point of involving his audience in the experience of travel, with personal anecdotes and interpolated images of trains. He also used dissolving sequences to add movement to key moments, like the death of Christ in his lecture on the Oberammergau Passion Play.

Stoddard's successor on the American circuit, E. Burton Holmes, was one of the first travel lecturers to introduce moving pictures into his lantern lectures in 1897. He also coined the term 'travelogue' (in 1904) for his hybrid slide-film lectures, which became the common term for travel films. But the early film producers already shared the same assumptions. Faced with the challenge of satisfying a sudden demand for film 'subjects' they turned first to the catalogues of other recent photographic media. Robert Paul's 14-part series, *A Tour Through Spain and Portugal* (1896) sounds exactly like a complete lantern travel lecture with the advantage of moving pictures. And as the Lumière catalogue grew to over 2,000 titles by 1903, it retained the same country headings, interspersed with 'vues comiques'

and miscellaneous subjects, as any nineteenth-century lantern slide or postcard supplier.

The Magic Lantern had created a taste for projected images, a form of optical theatre, which would help cinema become established as its successor. But there was another distinctive branch of nineteenth-century show business which dealt in 'reality'—suitably organised and classified according to much the same principles as the lantern-slide catalogues. When Prince Albert launched the 1851 Great Exhibition in London, he intended it to be a celebration of British achievement and an encouragement to substitute trade for war. He could hardly have known it would so catch the mood of the era—attracting six million visitors—that exhibitions would flourish, especially in France and the United States, as a novel forum to celebrate 'progress'.

Exhibitions combined the appeal of collecting, classifying, shopping, boasting, and tourism—all within increasingly fantastic buildings which began to resemble grown-up dolls' houses. A generation was stunned by the Great Exhibition's glass palace—Dostoevsky thought it 'like a Biblical picture, a prophecy coming to pass before your eyes'—and the Paris Exposition of 1889 celebrated the new age of electricity with the futuristic Eiffel Tower as its centrepiece. Ancient crafts and recently conquered 'natives' were displayed as living museum-pieces. Pavilions in exotic 'national' styles launched new cults of tradition alongside inventions that promised

NEXT WEEK!! at THE EMPIRE,
Once Again at Great Expense,
THE ORIGINAL
. UNSURPASSED .
UNEQUALLED
. LUMIERE .
CINEMATOGRAPHE
From the Empire, London,
Under the Direction of M. TREWEY.
A Series of Brilliant and Interesting Scenes absolutely true to life in
PRECISION, PROPORTION AND MOTION.
Towerskay in Moscow.
Children—Cat and Dog.
The Disappointed Artist.
Burmese Dance at the Crystal
Palace.
Hamburg Bridge, Germany.
A Remarkable Picture —
Soldiers' Parade in Madrid.
Concorde Bridge, Paris.
Lancers in Stuttgart.
Artillery in Barcelona.
Fire Brigade Call, London.
Charge of Cavalry in France.
AND
"TOBOGGANING IN SWITZERLAND."

to shrink the world. Verne's *Around the World in Eighty Days* was invoked in Paris in 1889—do it in six hours instead of 80 days on the Champ de Mars!

The exhibitions took themselves seriously, but they had more in common with humbler forms of entertainment than might have been admitted. When Phineas T. Barnum opened his American Museum in New York in 1842 with such attractions as the 'Feejee Mermaid', he invited the public to 'judge for itself' if this was 'a work of nature or a work of art'. The answer was not in doubt, but Barnum was catering to the same curiosity that would soon attract casual customers to the moving picture shows, and in the process establishing a new, democratic style of publicity which would become synonymous with the movies. Barnum and Prince Albert—the prince of humbug and the very model of a modern prince—were in reality two sides of the same Victorian coin. Both catered to a hunger for the fantastic and the exotic, masquerading as education and self-improvement.

As spectacles, the exhibitions were forerunners of what cinema would soon dispense to far-flung spectators; and the fantastic villages and cities built for them (a 'history of human habitation' in Paris in 1889) look like nothing so much as film sets waiting for the belated invention of cinema.

The 1893 Columbian Exposition in Chicago celebrated 400 years of American 'progress', and stimulated Edison to try to have his Kinetoscope ready for demonstration. In the event, he failed—although the stand and publicity stood waiting throughout—and it was the 1900 Universal Exposition in Paris, a birthday party for the start of the new century, which first featured moving pictures.

Moving pictures were already four years old as a public entertainment when the Exposition placed them in Group 3, Class 12 of its catalogue, between typography and assorted uses of printing, including sheet music. Film was indeed most obviously a means of recording and replaying—like its near-contemporary the player piano, which reproduced performances from a roll of punched paper. It was by no means the only novelty of 1900, but it featured in a total of eighteen exhibits at the exposition.

The contrast in attitude of the acknowledged pioneers, Edison and Lumière, could not have been greater. Edison had been the hero of Paris in 1889, feted for the phonograph and his association with everything electrical. But now his moving picture business was in the doldrums, hampered by sluggish production and lively competition. Paris 1900 was an opportunity to replenish the catalogue with some novel items, and two cameramen duly crossed the Atlantic to film the wonders of the exposition—a moving pavement, the Palace of Electricity and of course the Eiffel Tower.

Louis Lumière was a member of the exposition's organising committee and his company took joint responsibility for one of the most spectacular displays. This was a giant screen, sixty-five feet wide and moistened by fountains to make it translucent and visible from both sides, on which a programme of Lumière films and colour slides was shown throughout the exposition. Over six months, this changing programme was seen by nearly 1.5 million

Léon Gaumont

The company that Léon Gaumont (1864–1946) founded in 1896, together with its arch-rival Pathé, gave France an early lead in the international film industry. And Gaumont's near-obsession with adding sound to image helped keep this idea alive through much of the 'silent' period. Gaumont was a photographic supplier when Georges Demenÿ offered him a new moving picture mechanism. This had resulted from Demenÿ's work with Marey in the early 1880s and his efforts to build a machine for teaching the deaf to speak.

In 1896, Gaumont bought Demenÿ's patent and launched his first Chronophotograph projector-cum-camera. Needing films to encourage sales of the machine, and little interested in such matters, he put his secretary Alice Guy in charge of production. Still preoccupied with sound, he demonstrated the Chronophone system of performers miming to pre-recorded sound in 1902, and from 1905 the resulting 'Phonoscènes' featured regularly in Gaumont's growing cinema network.

Gaumont had started to expand early, opening a London branch in 1898 and others in Berlin, Moscow and New York. He built a major Paris studio in 1905, with advanced lighting and sound equipment, started a weekly newsreel in 1910 and introduced the Chronochrome colour process, which was triumphantly combined with sound in special programmes from 1912 at the flagship Gaumont Palace cinema in Paris.

Gaumont only survived the eclipse of French by American cinema thanks to its tireless new head of production, Louis Feuillade, whose *Fantômas* and subsequent mystery serials remained popular for nearly a decade. In 1924 Gaumont came effectively under MGM's control, but was still able to produce the first French sound feature in 1928 before its founder retired the following year.

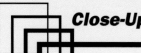

Charles Pathé

A 1908 French poster shows Charles Pathé (1863–1957) and his brother Emile striding forward with projector and phonograph under the slogan 'Towards the Conquest of the World'. This was no idle boast. Within two years, the former travelling showman would control nearly a quarter of the world's film trade.

Pathé had started in 1894 in fairgrounds with an Edison phonograph. He was soon importing these. Then he bought Paul's version of the Kinetoscope and had this adapted to sell as the Pathé Kinetograph. A camera followed, and in 1899 Pathé-Frères, as the company had become, started making films.

Ferdinand Zecca's arrival in 1901 signalled a more active production policy, aiming to supply all the kinds of film currently in demand—biblical, crime, comedy, magic, scenic—and to expand this range, as with their 'bawdy scenes'. Soon new studios at Vincennes and Montreuil catered for intensive assembly-line production.

In 1903, Pathé started opening foreign 'exchanges' to sell its films and equipment. Soon these circled the globe and often—as in Russia—also stimulated local production. In 1907 Pathé unilaterally decided to replace film sales by rental, forcing the whole industry to follow suit. Stencilled colour was a Pathé speciality from 1905, and in 1908 the *Pathé-Journal* became the world's first regular film newsreel.

Pathé-Frères eventually faced the same pressure from America as all other European film companies. In response to this, Charles Pathé went to America in 1913 to supervise his company's US branch. Ironically, the imports which later damaged French production were such US Pathé serials as *The Exploits of Elaine* (1915). After the First World War, Pathé began to break up his empire and he retired in 1929.

spectators. But it marked the climax of the Lumière involvement with what Louis had always believed to be 'an invention without a future'. Within five years, they would cease manufacture of the Cinématographe and sales of films, concentrating instead on their Autochrome colour photography process.

The dreams that inspired others exhibiting in 1900 were all of greater realism, or at least—since terms like 'realism' and 'naturalism' were hotly contested then, as now—of a more complete illusion. Among several 'environmental' uses of moving pictures, Raoul Grimoin-Sanson's Cinéorama was the most ambitious. This involved reproducing the experience of a balloon trip by having ten cameras film during a real ascent, then projecting the results (hand-coloured for greater realism) from ten projectors mounted centrally on to a vast wrap-around polygonal screen, while the audience watched from a mocked-up balloon basket. Astonishingly, Grimoin-Sanson succeeded in mounting this and the first screenings were reported 'an undeniable success'. But with the Charity Bazaar disaster still fresh in many memories, the police closed the Cinéorama as a fire risk on the same day it opened.

Adding sound to moving pictures had been on the agenda for more than a decade—indeed it was the success of his phonograph that first prompted Edison to try to record images. Several exhibitors claimed in 1900 to have solved the technical problems of synchronising the filmstrip and recording cylinder. The Phono-Cinéma-Théâtre offered an imposing array of brief performances by leading stage stars of the day, including Sarah Bernhardt as *Hamlet* and Coquelin in *Cyrano*. *Le Figaro* greeted this as 'a dream come true', but attendances were disappointing, as they were also for the Phonorama and the Théâtroscope. Even the large attendance for the Lumière giant screen was dwarfed by 2.7 million visiting the Hall of Illusions, which housed a light and mirror show.

Giant Lumière screen at the 1900 Paris Exposition

As a spectacle in their own right, moving pictures failed at the 1900 exposition. The efforts to add colour and sound may have seemed primitive compared with the more elaborate entertainments on offer. Yet such experiments would continue. Léon Gaumont, in particular, doggedly pursued sound and colour, producing hundreds of opera and music-hall 'phonoscènes' between 1904 and 1912. Also in 1904, Edison fulfilled his original prediction that the union of phonograph and kinetoscope would allow future generations to enjoy

grand opera being given at the Metropolitan Opera House in New York ... with artists and musicians long dead

when he authorised an expensive thirty-minute film of Wagner's sacred music drama *Parsifal*, indirectly based on a Met production. This was equipped with an accompanying lecture and could also be synchronised with recordings, but it did not sell.

The moving picture pioneers of 1900 were in thrall to what André Bazin would later call 'the myth of total cinema', dedicated to creating an 'illusion of life'. But what would secure the future of cinema as a global industry was something different. It was first an *intensification* of life, which would draw the spectator into an imaginary version of the 'real' world. While the pioneers of 1900 dreamed of 'progress' and film's role in achieving it, audiences were fascinated by the here and now of actuality.

Did it matter that the majority of early 'topicals' were not also 'actualities'? With the Spanish–American and Boer wars dominating public attention in the United States and Britain, there was a felt need to respond with relevant moving pictures. Initially these took the form of parades and troop embarkations. But what about the military action itself? Even when intrepid cameramen like William Paley (for Edison in Cuba) and Joe Rosenthal (for Urban in South Africa) travelled to the front line, their results, although popular, were often less impressive

Alice Guy directing an operatic Gaumont 'phonoscène' ca. 1904

than skilled illustrators could produce on the basis of eye-witness reports. The immediate solution was to stage typical scenes specially for the camera, either well behind the lines, as in Paley's *Shooting Captured Insurgents* (Edison, 1898), or simply at home, as Paul did in his 'Reproductions of Incidents of the Boer War'.

More dramatically, the Boer War was refought in Earls Court as *Savage South Africa—Attack and Repulse* (Warwick, 1899), by Mr Frank E. Fillis's troupe, 'as performed at the Empress Theatre "Greater Britain Exhibition"'; and near Orange, New Jersey, in *Capture of a Boer Battery by the British* (Edison, 1900), where kilted 'Highlanders' overcame the 'Boer' artillerymen. In *Boer Attack on a Red Cross Outpost* (1900), the propaganda stakes were raised when a Boer infiltrator throws a bomb at a hospital tent and injures a nurse.

It is easy to patronise the spectators of 1900 by assuming that most did not realise they were being deceived. But this is to forget the wider context of popular reporting and comment, in which film as yet played only a small part. It is also to assume a forensic view of authenticity which may itself be somewhat naive. Consider, for instance, one of the most famous early cases of supposed faking.

As the Lumière operators travelled far and wide with the Cinématographe, one of them, Francis Doublier, found himself in the Jewish districts of Southern Russia, where interest in the the Dreyfus Affair was high. Doublier decided to improvise and, according to his much later account, was soon able to present a 'Dreyfus film':

Joe Rosenthal filming in South Africa during the Boer War

We got out a film of some French officers marching. We pointed to one of the officers and said 'There is Dreyfus'. We showed an old picture of a French public building and said, 'There is the Palais de Justice where Dreyfus was court-martialled'. We showed a little boat going out to a warship, and shouted 'See! They are taking him to Devil's Island'. Then we showed a picture of a little island, and said, 'There is where they took him, Devil's Island'. The customers shed tears.

Does this simply mean that all or most of the Russian audience were taken in by Doublier's identification of the shots he showed? Or could it equally point to the audiences of 1900 having a different relationship to images? When *The Illustrated Police News* ran lurid engravings of the

Whitechapel Murders, the public naturally knew that these were what we would call 'an artist's impression'. They literally served to illustrate a story printed in detail, giving it dramatic form—and clearly drawing on the conventions of contemporary stage melodrama to do so.

We instinctively think of photography as breaking this dubious tradition and substituting 'true' images, but of course it did not do so for many years. So photographs (which were not reproduced in newspapers until well *after* 1900) and moving pictures started by functioning as illustration to what were still predominantly verbal narratives. Many in Doublier's audience would certainly have realised that Dreyfus had not been photographed during his ordeal. But they could still appreciate a 'typical' visualisation with film instead of drawings or slides. And yet, the portrayal of topical drama also needed new strategies of filming.

The Dreyfus Affair had raised such passions that Méliès produced his own dramatisation of it in 1899, based on newspaper photographs and reports for maximum accuracy, and issued as a series of twelve films lasting an unprecedented total of fifteen minutes. In one of these, *The Battle of the Journalists*, Méliès' concern with 'realism' led him to break all his own rules of filming,

allowing the seething court-room crowd to loom close to the camera and fill the frame in what looks to us like a startlingly modern piece of reportage. Suddenly, even today, we find ourselves in the picture.

In England, James Williamson dramatised an episide from the Boxer Rebellion as *Attack on a China Mission* (1901) 'on location' in Brighton. To enhance this drama of a missionary family under attack, he cut to a view taken in the opposite direction of a squad of marines arriving in the nick of time to rescue them. It is one of the earliest cases of what today would be called a 'reverse shot', and it involves us in the crossfire of the battle, placed there in a new kind of dramatic space created by film.

The public of the new century was experiencing a media revolution with cheap newspapers, photography and moving pictures all becoming affordable for large numbers in the industrialised

'The Battle of the Journalists' from *The Dreyfus Affair* (Méliès, 1899)

countries. Paid holidays were another novelty starting to spread and create new opportunities for travel—which an emerging tourist industry was ready to serve. Ever since Thomas Cook opened his travel agency in 1841 recreational travel had steadily become more accessible and popular. A Pathé film of 1907, *Spanish Postcard Views*, shows the tourist sights of Spain as a set of colour postcards that 'come to life' in a shop in the Alhambra. But even earlier, tourists started to appear in the actualities and 'interest' films of foreign sights.

A series photographed by Edison's European representative Alfred Abadie in 1903 follows a real tour around the Mediterranean in stages: *Tourists Landing at Capri/Returning on Donkeys from Mizpah/Starting on Donkeys for the Pyramids of Sakkarah/Taking Water from the River Jordan*. The audience, who might themselves be tourists, now wanted involvement. And the rituals of tourism were familiar enough to be satirised in a broad comedy like Porter's *European Rest Cure* (Edison, 1904), in which Joseph Hart plays a crusty old man sent on a cruise by his family. Using a combination of travel actuality and sets representing familiar Italian and Egyptian sites, this establishes beyond doubt that tourism was no longer the preserve of the very rich. Railway companies and tour operators also realised the importance of moving pictures to advertise their services and became active sponsors of films made among destinations they served.

Non-fiction films would continue to hold their place in all cinema programmes until the early 1910s, when longer 'feature' films began to dominate.

Indeed, the distinction between fiction and non-fiction was frequently blurred. 'Interest' films often had simple narratives and included staged incidents, while dramatic titles could also include actuality.

Meanwhile, filming itself was becoming a social and even an ethical issue. One of the strangest of early British films, Williamson's bizarre *A Big Swallow* (1901), shows a man speaking vigorously as the camera comes rapidly closer to his face and finally disappears into his mouth, leaving the screen black. It looks as if the man has swallowed it—and this turns out to be exactly what is intended, as Williamson's original catalogue entry explains:

'I won't! I won't! I'll eat the camera first'. Gentleman reading, finds a camera fiend with his head under a cloth, focusing him up. He orders him off, approaching nearer and nearer ... until his head fills the picture, and finally his mouth only occupies the screen. He opens it, and first the camera, then the operator disappear inside. He retires munching him up and expressing his great satisfaction.

The 'camera fiend' was already a recognisable social menace. Now moving pictures threatened a further, more radical, invasion of privacy.

Even filming with a manifestly serious purpose could raise wide alarm, as a French scandal proved. Shortly after the Lumière debut, the noted surgeon Eugène-Louis Doyen was struck by the idea of using cinematography to teach operating technique to medical students. He hired the Lumière operator who had organised their first public presentations, Clément-Maurice, to film a number of his operations and showed these at a medical congress in Edinburgh in 1898. His French colleagues were apparently outraged by this breaching of professional secrecy and forbade Doyen to show his films on medical occasions.

However Doyen soon became more widely known when a film of his operation in 1902 to separate the Siamese twins Radica and Doodica was found to be circulating among fairground freak-shows. Unknown to him, his assistant cameraman had printed up dozens of copies of the film and was doing a brisk illicit trade. Doyen successfully prosecuted his ex-assistant, although he wondered what objection there could be to better informing the public:

Is it regrettable, at a time when all classes of society are following with an interest amounting to passion the progress of surgery, that the non-medical public should be informed more exactly than by inadequate descriptions what a good operation is?

Five years later, a British doctor also raised professional

Doyen's film of his 1902 operation to separate Siamese twins

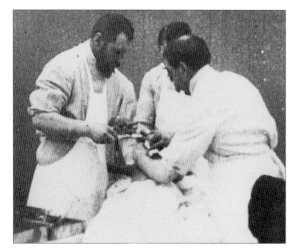

eyebrows when he illustrated his lectures with commercially-made films, although there were pioneering films of medical record elsewhere, such as the series of nine studies of epilepic seizures made in New York in 1905. But even aside from professional conservatism, film undoubtedly still had a fairground association, and its serious use for medical purposes may have been hampered by the popularity of crudely comic 'surgery' films—mainly fantasies of gruesome mistakes and casual dismemberment—such as those mentioned in the last chapter.

There were less provocative scientific worlds waiting to be explored through film, using it as—in Emmanuelle Toulet's phrase—a 'collective microscope'. Lantern slides taken through the microscope were already a familiar entertainment. With moving images, the microscopic world came to life and its viewers became explorers. Urban's 'Unseen World' series was launched in 1903, with twenty titles covering such subjects as *Birth of a Crystal*, *Cheese Mites*, *Circulation of Blood in the Frog's Foot* and *Anatomy of the Water Flea*.

Despite such uncompromising titles, Urban's films proved popular. The idea that even insects lived in societies with rules as complex as those of humans was attracting wide interest. And the Nobel Prize-winning dramatist Maurice Maeterlinck had an international success with his essays *The Life of the Bee* (1901) and *The Intelligence of Flowers* (1907). Now, through cinema, it was possible to discover *Nature's Hidden Beauties* (Britain, 1908) and enjoy *Peeps into Nature's Realm* (Britain, 1909). The

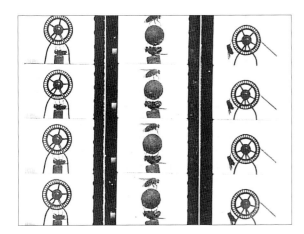

language of the titles constantly evokes the penetration of secrecy—a strange counterpart to the Victorian and Edwardian adventure fantasies by Rider Haggard and Conan Doyle of magical 'lost worlds'.

Yet there was little solemnity in early cinema, and natural history films, like every other genre, were also targets for mockery. Hepworth's *The Unclean World* (1903) gleefully parodies the 'Unseen World' series with a scientist inspecting his food through a microscope and discovering two large insects—which turn out to be clockwork toys when large hands appear to rewind them.

One remarkable Russian film-maker managed to combine the scientific with the parodic. Wladislaw Starewicz was a young naturalist and amateur photographer living in what is now Lithuania in 1909. He first used film to record insect behaviour, but when one of his subjects in *The Battle of the Stag Beetles* (1910) died under the lights, Starewicz completed the film by means of sealing wax and plasticine. He never returned to live-action entomology, but with the backing of Russia's leading

producer at the time, Khanzhonkov, made a series of allegorical and satirical masterpieces with insect puppets. *The Beautiful Lukanida* (1911) was the story of Helen and Paris, while a version of Krylov's fable, *The Ant and the Grasshopper* (1911), won the approval of the Tsar and wide international distribution.

Starewicz's satires, which he would later continue in French exile after 1917, started with *The Cameraman's Revenge* (1911). This translates a racy tale of double adultery into a startlingly modern world of insects, with the deceived husband a beetle cameraman and his rival a grasshopper painter. When the cameraman tries to make up with his unfaithful wife by taking her to the cinema, the film they see is of his philandering with a dragonfly, shot by the rival film-maker! To add even greater realism, a fire breaks out in the projection box as the beetle attacks his rival.

Sequences from The Physical Energy of the Fly (Percy Smith)

The Cameraman's Revenge (Starewicz, 1911)

Six days of a
flower's growth
'magnified' in
Percy Smith's
Birth of a Flower
(1911)

To hold an audience, film had to find a story, unless it borrowed one from fiction. But the act of filming could itself create or reveal a story. Time-lapse photography, or 'speed magnification' as it was known at the time, was the technique of taking single frames intermittently over a long period. When projected at normal speed, the results could be unexpectedly dramatic: animals hatching, plants germinating and sprouting. The growth of roses had been studied in France in this way as early as 1896, and ten years later a Mrs Scott showed her time-lapse films to the Royal Horticultural Society.

Speed magnification combined with colour made Percy Smith the undisputed leader in nature films after 1908. Like Starewicz, Smith had been an amateur photographer and naturalist. Frustrated by

failing to interest his employers, the Board of Education, in the new medium, he met Charles Urban, who was looking for ways to promote the Kinemacolor process. Smith developed his own special equipment for time-lapse cinematography and made *Birth of a Flower*, which was an acclaimed colour release in 1911. Over fifty natural history subjects followed before the war in Smith's 'Secrets of Nature' series.

Urban had realised before most that there was a vast appetite for stories of the real world waiting to be stimulated. This was not only for stories of the natural world; it was also a curiosity about the man-made world of industry, in which a growing proportion of the cinema's audience worked.

Of course, other people's work could be intriguing—if you lived far enough away, or it was very different from your own. When Pathé established a branch in Russia, they could be sure that even the sturdy women salting fish in a *Factory in Astrakhan* (1908, from the series 'Picturesque Russia') would seem exotic to French viewers. Indeed it would have been as exotic to the fashionable audiences of Moscow and St Petersburg as in London or Paris. But did audiences *really* want to see the inside of a factory close to home?

Apparently they did, and soon new specialised producers joined Pathé, Gaumont and Biograph in chronicling the changing face of industry in the new machine age. The publicity value of films showing modern manufacture led to early sponsorship by companies. The Library of Congress has a series of nineteen films made in 1904 which cover in great

Charles Urban

The American Charles Urban (1871–1942) was the super-salesman of early cinema and pioneer of international distribution. He started as a book agent in the Midwest before selling phonographs led him to moving pictures. Discovering that Edison's original projector was unsuited to rural use, Urban developed a practical adaptation which he marketed in 1897 as the Urban Bioscope.

His success brought an offer to manage an American company's London branch, which in 1898 Urban renamed the Warwick Trading Company. He became the British agent for Lumière and Méliès, as well as distributing Smith's and Williamson's Brighton production and later Vitagraph's output. In 1900, he sent operators to cover the Boer War, then to India and Abyssinia, and on a special Alpine expedition in 1902.

In 1903, Urban left Warwick to trade under his own name and concentrate on non-fiction, specialising in microscopic studies (Martin-Duncan's 'Unseen World' series) and 'interest' films from around the world. His 1908 catalogue, *Urbanora, the World's Educator*, celebrated an impressive international business and a shrewd vision of film's future.

Colour was a longstanding interest, and after his first researcher died in 1902, Urban encouraged G. A. Smith to work on what eventually became Kinemacolor. By 1910 the Natural Colour Kinematograph Company had a nationwide network of local franchise holders and studios in Brighton and the south of France. International expansion followed. But after legal challenges to his monopoly in 1913–15, Urban returned permanently to the United States, where his last reported activity was directing popular science features in the early 1920s.

Georges Méliès

Unlike many cinema pioneers, Georges Méliès (1861–1938) was quick to see the medium's potential. He attended the first Lumière public show in 1895 and immediately offered to buy a Cinématographe. When Antoine Lumière refused, Méliès promptly bought a projector from Paul and some Edison Kinetoscope loops. In April 1896 he began showing these loops at his Robert-Houdin Theatre in Paris.

Méliès had already spent a formative year in London in 1884, ostensibly to learn English before entering the family business. In England, he had discovered magic, as it was then performed on the London stage, and this led directly to his acquisition in 1888 of the Robert-Houdin. Once started with moving pictures, he soon designed a camera and began making his own films.

By 1897, he had built a studio at Montreuil and was selling his productions. These developed rapidly from simple actualities to 'assisted' conjuring tricks like *A Vanishing Lady* (1896), then to elaborate fantasies such as *The Temptation of St Anthony* (1898), and finally to faked newsreel (*The Dreyfus Affair*, 1899) and Vernean science-fiction (*Journey to the Moon*, 1902).

Méliès drew on the full array of Parisian stagecraft for his studio production, supplemented by ingenious stop-action and multiple exposure film techniques. His 'Star Films' soon had a world market and were widely pirated. Production averaged 20–30 titles per year until 1908, when declining business forced Méliès to reduce output. In 1912, he left cinema and tried a variety of unsuccessful theatre ventures over the next decade. Almost forgotten, Méliès was 'rediscovered' in 1929 in time to be honoured as the father of fantasy film.

detail the various manufacturing activities of the Westinghouse works in Pennsylvania. In Britain, *A Visit to Peek Frean and Co.'s Biscuit Works* was sponsored by that company in 1906 as publicity and helped set a pattern for films that followed raw materials through to finished products.

In Britain, as elsewhere, the stories most told were simple enough: the stages by which something common is manufactured in *Matches, Made in England* (1910) and *Making Christmas Crackers* (1910); the mysteries of modern engineering in *How a Motor Bicycle Is Made* (1912) and *Birth of a Big Gun* (1908); and the ever-popular 'day in a life' of an industry or process, as in *A Day in the Life of a Coalminer* (1910) and *At Messrs. Pilkington's Glassworks* (1913). If this was the 'operational aesthetic' (mentioned in Chapter 3), then it was stripped of any sugar coating of fiction. They showed clocking in, the discipline of the assembly line, automation, the feel of modern factory life. In doing so, they bade farewell to Victorian artisanal life and ushered in the new gospel of industrial 'efficiency'.

Might these films have opened a new window in the school classroom? Ever since the 1890s there had been an idea in the air that the ultimate value of moving pictures was educational. There had been heady rhetoric about a new 'universal language', as well as frequent allusions to the potential revelation of time-travel. In 1908, Charles Urban turned such aspirations into the concrete form of his large catalogue of factual films, grandly titled *Urbanora, the World's Educator*. But in his adopted country at least he found few ready to take up the challenge.

The secretary of the National Education Association was comprehensively dismissive:

I very much doubt the value of bioscope pictures in education. A good teacher studies the different capacity of his class ... And this is possible when using pictures, diagrams or even lantern slides. But the mechanical, regular movement of a bioscope offers no such opportunity. To the mental strain on the backward part of a class, there is also to be added ... the strain and damage to the eyesight.

Film, it might be deduced from this, posed a double threat. It would erode the teacher's absolute authority and offer a pleasure considered incompatible with education. Never mind that there were already contemporary reports of cinema-going helping to cut down delinquency, the idea that it 'damaged the eyesight' reads today like clear evidence that it was perceived by many in authority as dangerously subversive.

None the less some lone voices in Britain continued to urge the value of films in schools. The scientist Sir Ray Lankester wrote in 1911:

they can give to large gatherings of people, with the greatest ease and absolute truthfulness, a real view of microscopic life, and enable everyone to have a true conception of what the microscopist and biologist are actually studying ... I look

forward to the provision, not later than next year, of a cinematograph lantern in every board school, and in every college classroom.

It would be many years before British education authorities answered this call. But elsewhere there was greater enthusiasm.

France's most eminent philosopher, Bergson, gave a press interview in 1914 in which he noted how the cinematograph had already helped painters and that César Franck was using it in his teaching at the conservatoire. His final verdict was as sweepingly positive as the British verdict quoted above had been negative:

the cinematograph, while amusing the crowds, is seriously helping and will help the intellectual, the artist, the historian and even the philosopher.

Elsewhere in Europe, an obscure Swiss priest had gathered one of the largest known early film collections between 1902 and 1911 to show to the youth of Basel before a full-time cinema was established in the city. The Abbé Joye's motives may have been mainly pastoral, but more than half his 1,500 films (now housed in Britain's National Film and Television Archive) were non-fiction and these clearly played a vital part in his mission to entertain as well as inspire.

There were some other far-sighted figures who understood the potential of the new medium. One of the first in public life was Theodore Roosevelt, remembered as the politician who awakened America to the twentieth century with his combination of an energetic foreign policy and the curbing of big business powers. Roosevelt was a virtuoso of modern public relations even when he was still Vice-President. Early in 1901, he inspired what is probably the first political satire on film, Edison's *Terrible Teddy, the Grizzly King*. This shows a burly rifleman hurrying through a forest (Roosevelt was already famous for his hunting) accompanied by two figures labelled 'My Press Agent' and 'My Photographer'. The Great Hunter then makes a ceremonial kill for the camera in what was to prove a prophetic image.

Later that same year, McKinley's assassination brought Roosevelt to the White House; and appropriately he can be seen in one of the Porter films of McKinley's funeral. For Roosevelt was to become the most filmed of all statesmen before the Great War, and the first to establish his own film library. His most dramatic starring role was as a big-game hunter when he invited the English cameraman Cherry Kearton to film his 1908 African expedition.

Exploration and its sporting off-shoot, big-game hunting, had been conspicuous forms of imperial display in the late nineteenth century. Now they had begun to mutate, developing a scientific justification: explorers carried out observations and collected specimens. They also started to bring back films. Expeditions provided ideal subjects for moving picture narrative, offering audiences a chance to experience vicariously the thrills of the veld and jungle, and the hardship of the desert and polar explorer. So after accompanying Roosevelt, Kearton went on to film elsewhere in Africa and in India, Borneo and South America, and his films soon became yet another prestige series for their distributor, Charles Urban.

By 1911–12, a symbiosis had developed. No expedition was complete without provision for its film record, while the public appetite for such films—often shown outside normal cinemas, but immensely popular—in turn gave explorers and hunters a new kind of celebrity.

Being a 'celebrity' was clearly going to mean appearing on screen. Over the first decade of the century there was a gradual shift from the more or less convincing 'reproduction' of major public events (such as Méliès' commission to fake a film of Edward VII's coronation) to authentic film coverage. When Louis Blériot made the first aerial crossing of the English Channel in 1909, he was filmed limping on crutches towards his aeroplane, which anecdotal detail gave Pathé's record of the event a new dimension. And it was in the following year that both Pathé and Gaumont launched their weekly 'newsreels', which compact form would soon drive almost all other kinds of factual film off the commercial screen.

Thanks to film, flyers and explorers were the new heroes—and the pre-sale of rights to film companies also helped to pay for their exploits. When Captain Scott started planning his second Antarctic

Herbert Ponting's record of the Scott Antarctic Expedition 1910–11

Expedition in 1909, he knew that photography would play a vital part. Shackleton had shown his Antarctic material that same year and all the explorers of recent years had returned with stills and film, though often of variable quality. Scott was persuaded to make photography a special department of the expedition, Gaumont bought exclusive rights to his material, and he was lucky enough to recruit Herbert Ponting to run it. Ponting was already a well-known travel and landscape photographer; but he had no prior experience of cinematography and had to seek special training from the camera manufacturer Alfred Newman before the expedition left in 1910.

Ponting won Scott's admiration for his tireless enthusiasm during the Antarctic winter they spent at base camp, photographing and filming constantly for six months. Ponting would later recall how Scott had joked shortly before setting off on the final stage of the expedition that he was looking forward to seeing the film at his local cinema.

The first instalment of Ponting's film, contracted to Gaumont, was shown in Britain at the end of 1911, when Scott and his comrades were already in difficulties on their final trek to the Pole. By the time the second instalment was shown in 1912, they were dead, although this was not discovered until months later. Ponting's stirring record and his devotion to preserving and re-presenting it—first in combined lantern-slide and film lectures from 1913, then in a monumental 1924 feature, *The Great White Silence* (no doubt encouraged by the recent success of Robert Flaherty's *Nanook of the North*), and finally in an oddly moving 1933 sound version, *90° South*—would serve as their memorial.

What Rosenthal, Kearton and Ponting had begun would continue in films of exploration, discovery and, often, reconstruction. Flaherty went to the South Seas for *Moana* (1926) and *Tabu* (1933), to Ireland for *Man of Aran* (1934) and to India for *Elephant Boy* (1937). Ernest Schoedsack and Merian C. Cooper made two vast tribal studies, *Grass* (1925) and *Chang* (1927), before adding a fantasy coda to the cinema of exploration with *King Kong* (1933). These grand narratives reminded the urbanised cinema audience everywhere of its roots, besides giving it a modern version of the epic.

The assassination in Sarajevo in August 1914, which finally precipitated a long-expected European war, was itself partly captured on film. Within just four years, the newsreel had become the common currency of 'factual' film. International, omnipresent, formulaic—a miniature, rigidly framed window on the world outside the cinema. But what did it mean to the first generation who experienced this replay of reality? Virginia Woolf, writing in the mid-twenties, recalled the impression left by the early 'topicals':

There is the King shaking hands with a football team; there is Sir Thomas Lipton's yacht; there is Jack Horner winning the Grand National. The eye licks it all up instantaneously, and the brain, agreeably titillated, settles down to watch things happening without bestirring itself to think.

Soon, in Woolf's conceit, the brain and eye together realised that these simple scenes were 'more real' than daily life. But what *kind* of reality? She concluded that early actuality film showed 'life as it is when we have no part in it'. Reality at a remove—the space to reflect upon it, rather than simply react?

This was the startling new perspective which a generation was given, and it would inspire another writer with an eye for modernity to build a whole novel around the idea of the camera's impassive stare. Luigi Pirandello is better known today for his classic *Six Characters in Search of an Author*, but in 1916 *The Notebooks of Serafino Gubbio* (also known as '*Shooting!*') was one of the first attempts to anatomise this new reality—the world as seen through a movie camera.

Wladislaw Starewicz

Born in Moscow in 1882 to a Polish family, Wladislaw Starewicz was brought up in Kovno, Lithuania, after his mother's early death. His early interests included drawing, model-making and magic lanterns, as well as the study of insects. After his marriage, he worked in the Kovno Treasury while continuing to practise photography and selling cartoons to earn extra money.

His talents came to the attention of Aleksandr Khanzhonkov, one of the new Russian producers who had emerged around 1908. Khanzhonkov backed him to make some natural history films. But in 1910 the difficulty of filming live insects drove Starewicz to experiment with model animation for *The Battle of the Stag Beetles*.

The result was so successful that he continued, in an increasingly fictional and fantastic vein, with *The Beautiful Lukanida*, *The Cameraman's Revenge* and *The Insects' Aviation Week* (all 1911). A fable, *The Ant and the Grasshopper*, was apparently one of the first Russian films to be exported. Starewicz moved to Moscow and, after providing animated segments for *Voyage to the Moon* and *The Evils of Alcohol* (both 1912), started working in live-action cinema. In 1913, he directed two feature-length Gogol adaptations, both full of magical effects and with the leading Russian actor of the period, Mozzhukin, *A Terrible Vengeance* and *Christmas Eve*.

Russia's entry into the First World War allowed Starewicz to return occasionally to animation for propaganda films like *Stepson of Mars* (1914) and *The Lily of Belgium* (1915); but it was not until the revolutions of 1917 forced him into exile that Starewicz returned to puppet animation, working prolifically near Paris from 1920 until his death in 1965.

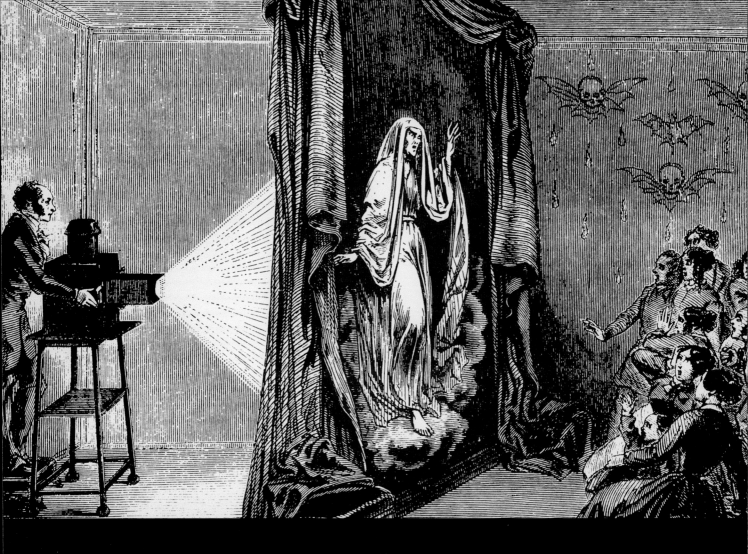

5 The Waking Dream

Horror movies predate the machinery of Edison and Lumière by at least a century. Indeed cinema might well be described as a temporary phase in the supernatural tradition which started as long ago as the seventeenth century and looks set to continue into the future with computer controlled 'virtual reality'.

The basic techniques of using shadows, noise, sudden movement and atmosphere to spook an audience were established during the eighteenth century. And the paraphernalia of ghosts, haunted ruins, nasty ways of dying and un-dying was already familiar by the beginning of the century that would produce such horror staples as *Frankenstein*, *Jekyll and Hyde* and *Dracula*. In fact the nineteenth century was as much under the spell of the occult as of any other passion. Everyone—royalty, priests, soldiers, scientists, merchants and ordinary people—seemed caught up in a collective 'will to believe'.

What did they want to believe? Essentially, that death was not final; that communication with 'the other side' was possible—from which it followed that one might see into the future, conjure spirits and even achieve immortality. So the respectable Victorians threw themselves into spiritualism, seances, tarot cards and magic of many kinds. In this climate, it was scarcely surprising that moving pictures seemed supernatural to their first viewers. Both the Paris newspapers which reported the first Lumière show ended their reviews on the same note:

... death will cease to be absolute.

... it will be possible to see our nearest alive again long after they have gone.

Even the hard-headed Edison, as we have seen, quite naturally imagined the future of his combined sound and picture recording in terms of 'artists and musicians long since dead'.

A hundred years earlier, Paris saw the appearance of two early spectacles that both played upon a public appetite for the eerie and the ghoulish. One was a development of the Magic Lantern, which already had a somewhat macabre reputation. From its beginnings a century earlier, some of the most common lantern images were skeletons, ghosts and devils. The very term 'magic' already linked the lantern with the black arts, and the fact that it required darkness no doubt encouraged such gruesome imagery. Lit by a flickering candle or oil lamp, the painted slides would have been highly effective.

Nothing like as effective, though, as the 'Phantasmagoria', which burst upon Paris in the late 1790s. This used a mobile lantern with a shutter, projecting from behind the screen. Displayed in a suitably atmospheric setting by its Belgian inventor (who called himself 'Robertson', perhaps because England had a 'Gothic' reputation), this created a sensation. A Scottish scientist later described the touring version by Philipstal which came to London and Edinburgh:

A spooky magic lantern show

MANNERS· AND· CVSTOMS· OF· Yͤ ENGLYSHE· IN 1849· Nº. 27.

Yͤ CELEBRATED MVRDERERS.

MADAME· TVSSAVD· her· WAX· WERKES.   Yͤ CHAMBER· OF· HORRORS.!!

Punch cartoon of Madame Tussaud's Chamber of Horrors (1849)

the curtain rose and displayed a cave with skeletons and other terrific figures in relief upon its walls. The flickering light was then drawn up beneath its shroud and the spectators in total darkness found themselves in the middle of thunder and lightning. A thin transparent screen had ... been let down after the disappearance of the light ... The thunder and lightning were followed by the appearance of ghosts, skeletons and known individuals, whose eyes and mouth were made to move by the shifting of combined sliders ... The head of [Benjamin] Franklin was transformed into a skull; figures which retired with the freshness of life came back in the form of skeletons ...

The exhibition of these transmutations was followed by spectres, skeletons and terrific figures, which ... suddenly advanced upon the spectators ... The effect of this part of the exhibition was naturally the most impressive. The spectators were not only surprised but agitated.

Robertson's shows took place less than a decade after the French Revolution, which may well have influenced his imagery—and had also inadvertently started another gruesome form of entertainment: the waxworks Chamber of Horrors. The future Madame Tussaud had served her apprenticeship modelling from life at the court of Louis XVI, before the Revolution obliged her to model the guillotined heads of her former friends.

When she moved to England in 1802, it was at the invitation of Philipstal, who had opened a 'Grand Cabinet of Optical and Mechanical Curiosities' in London. Here the phantasmagoria, a waxworks and a display of the equally fashionable 'automata', or early robots, were all at first exhibited together: a highly significant gathering of the cinema's three most impressive precursors in the field of simulation.

The same theatre also housed an exhibition called 'Egyptiana' which, in the wake of Napoleon's 1799 expedition to Egypt, would have recalled the links between the modern and the ancient occult. For Philipstal and his like were happy to hint at a secret tradition of esoteric mysteries, in which the Egyptian mummy figured as a popular symbol of the desire for immortality. Later the cinema would return frequently to this theme. An early example is *The Princess and the Vase*, a 1908 Biograph film in which D. W. Griffith plays an ancient Egyptian courtier who 'follows' his beloved to the present and, when she materialises out of a funeral vase, avenges himself on his modern rival the archaeologist.

Madame Tussaud soon separated her 'topical' figures from the gruesome relics of the revolutionary Terror, which included the heads of Robespierre and the executioner Fouquier-Tinville, and her full-scale tableau of Marat's death, to create what eventually became known as the Chamber of Horrors. This proved not only popular, but highly fashionable. It also inspired the recurrent fantasy—which no doubt explains its attraction—of seeing its wax figures come alive. The caricaturist Cruikshank published a cartoon in 1847, with a verse attached:

I dreamt that I slept at Madame Tussaud's
With cut-throats and Kings side by side:
And that all the wax figures in those abodes
At midnight became revivified.

Sixty years later, the young Sergei Eisenstein was taken to Paris by his parents and paid a 'never to be forgotten' visit to the Grévin wax museum. The future maestro of Soviet revolutionary cinema was an imaginative little boy from Riga already fascinated by images from French illustrated books and magazines. But at the Grévin museum these scenes took concrete form.

Early horror: an impression of Robertson's 'Phantasmagoria' in action

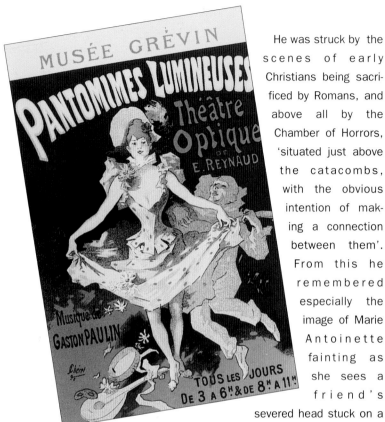

Poster for Reynaud's 'Optical Theatre' at the Grévin waxworks in Paris

He was struck by the scenes of early Christians being sacrificed by Romans, and above all by the Chamber of Horrors, 'situated just above the catacombs, with the obvious intention of making a connection between them'. From this he remembered especially the image of Marie Antoinette fainting as she sees a friend's severed head stuck on a pike carried past her cell window. When Eisenstein himself became a film-maker working in the aftermath of a revolution he was drawn to this same lurid tradition in the shocking images of violence he created for *The Battleship Potemkin* and later *Alexander Nevsky*.

Wax museums were as much a part of the nineteenth century's obsession with reproducing reality as were all its optical entertainments. And appropriately they were the scene of several important transitional experiments in the 1890s. Emile Reynaud ran his 'optical theatre' at the Grévin

museum for five years, until the fashionable (and labour-saving) new Lumière cinematograph put him out of business. Across the Atlantic, New York's equivalent establishment, the Eden Musée found itself with a similar problem in 1895. It had been one of the first exhibitors of the Kinetoscope, but Edison was failing to come up with attractive new film loops. In desperation, the manager of Edison's Kinetoscope department decided to adapt some traditional waxworks tableaux as moving pictures: *Joan of Arc*, *The Rescue of Captain Smith by Pocahontas*, *A Lynching Scene* and—the only one of these to survive—*The Execution of Mary Queen of Scots*.

The results were ahead of their time and pointed the way forward for future production, for these are embryonic adventure movies. What the Eden had done was to 'realise' the action implicit in static waxworks scenes. In *Mary Queen of Scots*, the blade appears to fall on the living queen, while—thanks to stop-action—a dummy head drops. Seen in the setting of a waxworks, even in the Kinetoscope peep-show, this effect would be even more startling.

The following year, 1896, moving pictures started to appear on screens everywhere. But they did not attract anything like the same attention as another scientific novelty of the time. Although X-rays had been developed by Wilhelm Röntgen for medical purposes, they were eagerly taken up by showmen as an intriguing new way of making a spectacle of the human body. The erotic implications were immediately obvious: X-rays could 'see through' clothes to reveal a bizarre form of nakedness. They also allowed people to see their own bones in an up-

G. A. Smith

George Albert Smith (1864–1959) was one of the Brighton-based English pioneers whose background in photography enabled him to build his own camera in 1896 and to begin selling films in the following year. An early interest in trick effects led Smith to patent the process of double-exposure used in his 1897 films *The Corsican Brothers*, *Photographing a Ghost* and *The Haunted Castle*.

In 1900, Smith formed a partnership with Charles Urban which allowed him to concentrate on research and production, leaving business to Urban. A studio was built in the same year, making possible more elaborate trick films like *Mother Goose Nursery Rhymes* (1902) and *Dorothy's Dream* (1903). Smith also introduced the big close-up into film in 1900 with *Grandma's Reading Glass* and *The Little Doctor*.

When Urban's first partner working on colour cinematography died, Smith took up the task. In 1906, he and Urban patented Kinemacolor, the first film system to give true colour (rather than artificially coloured) reproduction, by means of a rotating red and green filter in front of both camera and projector lens. It was widely demonstrated in 1908–9 with records of current events and Smith's film *Kinemacolor Puzzle*. State occasions, like the coronation of 1910 and the Delhi Durbar of 1912, as well as the striking changes then taking place in women's fashion, were popular colour subjects.

The Natural Colour Kinematograph Company released its first drama, *The Story of Napoleon*, in 1910 and expanded internationally. But its tightly-enforced monopoly was broken by a legal ruling in 1914 which effectively ended Smith's career in cinema.

Paul Wegener

Paul Wegener (1874–1948) was one of the first established actors anywhere to commit himself enthusiastically to cinema, at a time when it still seemed beneath the dignity of many in the theatre. He had been a leading member of Reinhardt's famous company in Berlin since 1906, but quickly understood that film should not merely reproduce theatre, either as a source or in its techniques. Instead he believed it was particularly suited to exploring the mythic, the supernatural and the subjective—as *The Student of Prague* (1913) triumphantly showed.

In 1914, he co-directed *The Golem*, a Jewish Frankenstein-like myth with which he would remain closely associated, collaborating on two later versions in 1917 and 1920. His other early films—mostly as actor and co-director and/or writer, for Wegener was an early film 'author'—also pursued supernatural themes. *Peter Schlemihl* (1915) acknowledged E. T. A. Hoffmann as an inspiration for this new kind of adult fairy tale, while *The Pied Piper of Hamelin* (1916) and *Hans Trutz in Sleepland* (1917) showed how children's stories could take on a new power on the screen.

When German Expressionist cinema became a major artistic and commercial success in the wake of *The Cabinet of Dr Caligari* (1919), it owed much to Wegener's pioneering example. He played the lead in Rex Ingram's 1926 French production *The Magician* (on which the young Michael Powell served his apprenticeship) and was still a leading actor-director when, from 1933, he lent his considerable prestige to the emerging Nazi cinema.

to-date form of the medieval 'momento mori', or intimation of mortality.

One of the many early X-ray shows deserves mention, since it shows how closely science and magic were woven together in the popular mind. Edison had played no part in developing X-rays, but he had an image as the scientific 'wizard' to live up to in the eyes of the American public. So in 1896, he announced a New York exhibition of his 'perfected' equipment. The setting that awaited visitors was described as:

Egyptian darkness lit only by two blood-red incandescent lamps, the rays of which were intercepted from the fluoroscope by pendant palls of black.

Reactions to the sight of their hand X-rayed varied from alarm to amusement, with a strong current of scepticism—and the fact that Edison himself often used to sit in the adjoining control room irresistibly recalls the denouement of Frank Baum's *The Wonderful Wizard of Oz* (1900) in which Oz the Terrible is revealed as a humbug cowering behind a screen.

Edison knew, like Oz, how to blend Barnum-style showmanship with new technology. X-rays tapped into a popular hunger for tangible signs of 'the other side'. In this, they followed the vogue for 'spirit photography', which owed much to a series of images taken in the 1870s by the distinguished English scientist and president of the Royal Society, Sir William Crookes. Some Victorian photographers already included absent or dead members of a family in their group portraits—presumably to show them present 'in spirit'. It was a short step for such practical mystics as Crookes and the creator of Sherlock Holmes, Arthur Conan Doyle, to seek photographic evidence of spiritual 'manifestation'.

Both spirit photography and X-rays soon found their way on to the other new medium which combined scientific and popular appeal. G. A. Smith was already a versatile Brighton photographer when he built his own moving picture camera in 1897 and started a career in trick double-exposure films. *The X-Ray Fiend* followed a frequent comic theme of the time, with a professor turning his new machine on a courting couple. And in the following year Smith tackled *Photographing a Ghost*, described in his catalogue as follows:

A Photographer's Studio. Two men enter with a large box labelled 'ghost'. The photographer scarcely relishes the order, but eventually opens the box, when a striking ghost of a 'swell' steps out. The ghost is perfectly transparent so that the furniture, etc, can be seen through his 'body'. After a good deal of amusing business with the ghost, which keeps appearing and disappearing, the photographer attacks it with a chair.

Unfortunately both films are lost, but a record survives of Smith selling his *X-Ray Fiend* for more than three times its production cost of 14 shillings to the leading magician David Devant.

Magicians, not surprisingly, were among the first to use trick films in their performances and some, like Méliès, went on to become full-time film-makers. Magic as a popular entertainment had also been infected by the new occult movement, with the Davenport Brothers claiming to be 'American spiritualist mediums'. This in turn provoked a reaction, and two of England's most famous magicians, Maskelyne and Cooke, emerged in the 1860s with an act which deliberately revealed the Davenports' faking. And it was their mixture of classic illusionism, exposés of fradulent seances and 'magnetism', and comic sketches that inspired Méliès.

He was in London in 1884, ostensibly to learn English and gain experience for his family's bootmaking business. But he spent his evenings at the Egyptian Hall in Piccadilly where Maskelyne and Cooke performed as 'Royal Illusionists and Anti-Spiritualists'. Méliès started to study magic, attending Robert-Houdin's Theatre of Illusions when he returned to Paris. He began to perform himself, both privately and at the Grévin museum. By 1888, he had extricated himself from the family business and was able to buy the Robert-Houdin when it came up for sale.

Over the next seven years, he developed a distinctive style of *scènes burlesques*, which, like Maskelyne and Cooke, placed classic and newly invented illusions in dramatic settings. He also continued the theatre's tradition of Magic Lantern shows, so that (as he noted in his third-person memoirs):

long before the cinema, Méliès was very familiar with projections properly so-called.

What he learnt were the basic devices of stop-action or substitution and multiple exposure of the same length of film. Armed with these, Méliès soon went beyond reproducing and embellishing magic tricks from the stage, such as *A Vanishing Lady at the Robert-Houdin* (1896), although he would periodically return to a stage setting for ever more elaborate tricks like *The Man with the India-Rubber Head* (1902).

Increasingly, Méliès turned his invention to creating fantastic worlds on film. Some of these were imagined versions of the real world, as in *The Dreyfus Affair* (1899), or *Volcanic Eruption in Martinique* and

1894 poster for a magic presentation at Méliès' Paris theatre anticipating many of the effects he would later achieve on film, as in right: *The Man with the India-Rubber Head* (1902)

The Man with the India-Rubber Head

The earliest extended narrative in cinema, as distinct from one- and two-shot anecdotes, was religious. At a time when many potential viewers were suspicious of fiction on principle and unfamiliar with its conventions, the only story that was universally known (at least in all the early film-producing countries) was the life of Christ. There were many precedents for this from other media. Over the centuries, the gospel story had been retold in stained glass, painting, sculpture, lithography; and more recently in waxworks, lantern slide and even photography.

It was photography that first threw up the basic theological problem which has continued to rear its head throughout this century (and caused lasting scandal around such films as *The Life of Brian* and *The Last Temptation of Christ*). How can a realist medium avoid giving offence by picturing what is normally not seen, or is at least always idealised in other media?

This was not a problem for the Roman Catholic cultures which had long sponsored religious painting and imagery of many kinds as an essential part of their culture. But it did perplex the Protestants of Northern Europe and North America, who had largely suppressed religious imagery since the Reformation. Hence the outrage that greeted photographic studies of the Christ made by the American aesthete

The Coronation of Edward VII (both 1902). But more often they were the worlds of pantomime, fairy tale and Vernean fantasy. Central to all of them was the idea of *transformation*—something or someone turning magically into something else—and often, in more than a hundred of his films, he himself played the agent of transformation: diabolic as the Devil, Mephistopheles or a sorcerer; or benign as simply a magician. In an era of 'magic' films, Méliès' had a quality and sheer invention that put them in a class of their own. But they all respected the stage-auditorium boundary; and the more elaborate and fantastic they became, the more theatrical they seemed to audiences who were learning a new 'realism' from other films. Ultimately, trans-formations proved no match for the appeal of storytelling.

Frederick Holland Day in the 1890s. Admittedly Day posed himself as the model, though he took punctilious care over authentic props. But the reaction was hostile. One magazine declared:

the living Jesus, with face illuminated by the Divine Inspiration, seems beyond the power of the camera.

A writer in the *British Journal of Photography* was more measured in his criticism:

As there are no originals left of sacred subjects, it seems to me there is no field for photography in this direction. In looking at a photograph, you cannot forget that it is a representation of something which existed when it was taken.

From this point of view, how could any photograph of a 'sacred' subject be other than, literally, blasphemous? The problem was never solved in Britain, which made 'materialism of Christ or the Almighty' one of the only two absolute grounds on which films could be banned by its first censor in 1913. Nor was it solved in Tsarist Russia, which also banned all religious imagery in films—a diktat which the Soviet regime effectively continued, for different reasons, while encouraging *anti*-religious propaganda in films.

But American showmen were not to be defeated so easily. The first solution was to make a film which quite explicitly did not pretend to show Christ, but used a non-professional actors portraying the gospel story in a traditional community passion play. In this way, the film put itself at one remove from the sacred story, as an of 'actuality' of a legitimate portrayal, and so avoided charges of irreverence or blasphemy.

Assuming, that is, it was a *real* passion play. The first such film was made at a village in Bohemia in 1897 and resulted in the relatively unspectacular *Horitz Passion*, which none the less alerted American exhibitiors to the potential of the subject. It prompted the president of the Eden Musée waxworks to back a much more lavish version, using costumes prepared seventeen years earlier for a New York stage production which had been banned at the last moment due to religious pressure on the mayor. The new passion film was made secretly at an improvised rooftop studio in New York in December—there are anecdotes of camels being smuggled up in freight elevators—and launched triumphantly in January 1898 as a record of the famous Oberammergau Passion Play.

Running for about twenty minutes (although lantern slides, music and a spoken text made the whole show two hours), the Eden presentation had an immediate success, not least with religious leaders and churchgoers. Even the revelation that it could not have been filmed at Oberammergau—since the last performance had taken place before moving pictures were invented!—could not dent its appeal. In its wake, passion films appeared on all sides, giving exhibitors a wide choice of style, and price. Lumière produced their thirteen-part series in 1898. One American producer offered a range of versions:

25, 20, 15, 12 or 9 parts. Pathé and later Gaumont regularly updated their popular passion series, which were attractively coloured by stencil from as early as 1902.

As exhibitors across the world chose from the numerous competing catalogues, they were also creating the first multi-scene film narratives that their audience would see. Many would no doubt have mixed episodes from different suppliers. Others, especially religious users, would have chosen the episodes according to their doctrinal preferences. As early as 1898, a pioneering American evangelist, Colonel Henry Hadley, proclaimed:

It is the age of pictures ... These moving pictures are going to be the best teachers and the best preachers in the history of the world ... Mark my words, there are two things coming: prohibition and moving pictures.

Moving pictures helped to modernise the message, or rather to suggest that it was still relevant to the modern world. Many religious film enthusiasts would probably have agreed with William Booth, who had launched the Salvation Army in 1878 with an emphasis on popular music-making, that 'the devil should not have all the good tunes.'

The Swiss Jesuit priest Joseph Joye has already been mentioned as a keen advocate of the new medium. Joye used his large collection to attract the youth of Basel to regular screenings, and like any experienced youth worker he knew not to preach too insistently. Roland Cosandey, the historian of this collection, estimates that less than 5 per cent of his films had any explicit religious content. But as Joye commented on and linked his films, like the lantern lecturer he had also been, he would undoubtedly have put them in a broadly Christian context. Cosandey speculates that he may well, for instance, have poured scorn on films like *The Human Ape* and *Darwin's Triumph*, since Evolution was still a lively popular controversy.

Early films could easily be presented—and received—in very different ways, and this was especially true of religious subjects. Another early cinema historian, Miriam Hansen, records that Vitagraph's five-reel *The Life of Moses* (1910) had a particularly enthusiastic response from Russian Jewish audiences in America, although it had been produced with impeccably Christian credentials. The fact that moving pictures had arrived at the peak of a worldwide religious revival meant that they were virtually bound to be caught up in its momentum, even if its various strands—from the social evangelism of Booth's Salvation Army, to the Catholic Revival and such mystical movements as Theosophy—would have very different attitudes towards this upstart.

After such pioneer religious exhibitors as Hadley and Joye, came the pioneer religious producers. Religious subjects led the trend towards even longer films at the start of the century's second decade; and even if, like the passion cycles, these were backward-looking in their sources, they did much to create the new dramatic language of cinema. The most ambitious was Kalem's *From the Manger to the Cross*, which ran an unprecedented 80 minutes when it was released to massive acclaim in 1912.

Although filmed 'on location' in Palestine, this drew heavily on a popular turn-of-the-century book, the 'Tissot Bible', for its adaptation of the Gospel story. James Tissot's sequence of illustrations had itself benefited from several expeditions to the Holy Land in the 1880s, but was often sentimental in its visualisations. However, once this 'storyboard' was filmed by Sidney Olcott and his team on many of the sites that had originally inspired Tissot, it became something different, as a recent historian suggests:

From the Manger to the Cross
(Olcott, 1912)

to have taken [Tissot's] *The Youth of Jesus*, **in which Mary and Joseph seem clandestine in observing the boy carrying a plank of lumber, and effected the shadow of the Cross as Jesus steps into the sunlight, is a genuine stroke of theatricality. The idea for the shadow came from another painting, Holman Hunt's** *The Shadow of Death* **... but in the boy's direct stare into the sun, Kalem contributes the intimation of a heavenly communion ...**

From the Manger to the Cross was (in modern terms) the first feature-length American film—the forerunner not only of later 'lives of Christ', but of many other aspects of cinema as spectacle and as a new kind of popular culture.

Many devout souls, in Britain as well as America, who would never have dreamed of entering a theatre or even reading a secular novel, were assured that this was truly 'reverent' and inspirational. Some would have gone on to see Charles Russell's apocalyptic *Photo-Drama of Creation* in 1914, an audiovisual extravaganza which in its longest version ran eight hours (five of slides, three of film), with synchronised speech and music on disc, and aimed to show nothing less than:

everything appertaining to the creation of earth—animals, man, the experiences of mankind for the past six thousand years and the work of the thousand years of Messiah's Kingdom.

Russell was a controversial leader of what would become the Jehovah's Witnesses and, like many evangelists, an intuitive media visionary. However overblown his anti-Darwinian 'photo-drama' may have been, it toured extensively for three years and reminds us of the extraordinary ambition that cinema already inspired.

The film that proved even more influential than these specifically religious subjects was an Italian adaptation of Henryk Sienkiewicz's immensely popular 1896 novel, *Quo Vadis?*. Italian cinema, as noted in Chapter 3, had already won international success with spectacles of the ancient world like *The Last Days of Pompeii* and *The Fall of Troy*. But *Quo Vadis?* overwhelmed audiences everywhere with its mighty sets, crowds, chariot race and the final massacre of the Christians by lions. This was what the young Eisenstein and countless others around the world had imagined, and seen as waxworks tableaux, but never on the scale of Guazzoni's film.

Anecdotes of its impact abound, many of them hard to verify. The sculptor Rodin apparently declared it a 'masterpiece'. King George V is said to have congratulated its athletic star, Bruto Castellani, the first of many movie musclemen. And when it opened for an exclusive run at the Astor Theatre on Broadway, the *New York Times* ended its admiring review with a prediction:

The acting of the principals was calculated to help the illusion at all times, and the handling of the small army of supernumeraries admirable. If a feature moving-picture production can fill a Broadway theatre, *Quo Vadis?* ought to be able to do it.

It did—and ran for twenty-two weeks, leaving at least one American film-maker determined that he would make something as spectacular. To the dismay of his employers, D. W. Griffith started building a large walled city set for what would be his longest film to date, the biblical tale *Judith of Bethulia* in four reels. The way had been opened to a home-grown epic, in Griffith's *The Birth of a Nation* (1915), and also to a moralised version of the Italian spectacular in his *Intolerance* (1916). Soon America would adopt the biblical epic as a genre peculiarly close to its collective conscience.

Quo Vadis?
(Guazzoni, 1912)

Religion, however, was not simply a matter of spectacle. Indeed the root of the Protestant suspicion of cinema, as of all visual media, lay in that tradition's denial of the visible as a 'distraction' of the senses. But although it seems natural to think of cinema as visual, and so committed to explicit 'showing', it soon became apparent that film could also deal with the 'invisible'.

For some of their first viewers, moving pictures seemed strangely close to other contemporary trends that were variously known as Decadence, Symbolism or even, as the new century approached, simply '*fin de siècle*'. What these shared was a turning away from realism and explicit meaning, towards more mysterious and suggestive strategies. In a 'Manifesto of Symbolism' published in France in 1886, the poet Jean Moréas wrote:

Symbolist poetry strives to invest the Idea with palpable form, which however is not a goal in itself, but should be subordinated to the Idea ... the essence of symbolic art lies in its never calling the Idea by its proper name.

This is the immediate background to one of the best-known of all early responses to the cinematograph, Maxim Gorky's 1896 article, part of which was quoted in Chapter 2:

Yesterday I was in the kingdom of the shadows.

If only you knew how strange it is to be there. There are no sounds, no colours. There,

everything—earth, trees, people, water, air— is tinted in the single tone of grey: in a grey sky there are grey rays of sunlight: in grey faces, grey eyes, and the leaves of the trees are grey like ashes. This is not life, but the shadow of life, and this is not movement but the soundless shadow of movement.

I must explain, lest I be suspected of Symbolism or madness. I was at Aumont's café and saw the Lumières' Cinémato-graphe—moving photographs.

It is a salutary shock, accustomed as we are to accounts of early film's realism, to find Gorky instinctively relating these 'grey shadows' to the Symbolist art that was attracting attention in the mid-nineties: the flat, monotone paintings of Puvis de Chavannes and Eugène Carrière in France, and in Russia the haunted, dream-like work of Mikhail Vrubel.

Oscar Wilde had written in *The Picture of Dorian Gray* (1891) that 'all art is at once surface and symbol', and among like-minded 'decadent' photographers of the time there is a fascination with the possibilities of hinting at what lies behind the apparently realist surface of the photograph. A self-portrait by Wilde's friend Frederick Holland Day from 1897 shows a ghostly black figure behind him, suggesting an alter ego or perhaps even an erotic fantasy. And is *Dorian Gray* itself not an uncanny anticipation of cinema's ability to 'freeze' time, as Dorian remains perpetually young while all around him grow old? The implied effect is that of watching

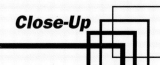
D. W. Griffith

David Wark Griffith was born in Kentucky in 1875, and it was only after ten dispiriting years as a struggling actor and writer, that he started to work in films in 1907. In the following year, he began directing for Biograph and started to develop what can only be called a personal vision. The Bible, popular literary classics, songs and newspaper headlines were all grist to his weekly mill. These mainly one-reelers, lasting no more than twelve minutes, drew on the whole culture of America to explore how the ways of God and man could be reconciled, as traditional country values met the new urban and industrial challenges.

The world of these films is intensely moral: a gloating Wall Street broker is buried in the grain elevator which a poor farmer helps to fill (*A Corner in Wheat*, 1909); an outraged father ambushes his daughter's seducer, only for him to die of a heart attack (*Heaven Avenges*, 1912). But its fatalism is tempered by sentimentality, as parents and children are regularly reconciled after years of separation, and lovers tragically parted by death. Nor is it without humour and a touch of the fantastic—as when a woman at the movies with a big hat is suddenly snatched upwards by a mechanical excavator in *Those Awful Hats* (1909).

Billy Bitzer's plain photography and the relatively sober acting style Griffith cultivated help to suggest strong emotions and beliefs that are held in check until moments of catharsis or epiphany. Even before the self-conscious epics of *The Birth of a Nation* (1915) and *Intolerance* (1916), his Biograph films are the twentieth-century equivalent of the great medieval story collections. He died in 1948.

August Blom

August Blom (1869–1947) was one of the Danish film-makers who owed his career to the remarkable success of the Nordisk company. Founded in 1906, Nordisk expanded rapidly and was soon producing and exporting over a hundred films a year, specialising in literary adaptation, broad comedy and 'sensation' films.

Blom had been a theatre actor before starting to write and direct for Nordisk in 1906. He soon graduated to prestige productions with a *Hamlet* shot on location at Elsinore in 1910. In the same year, he discovered Asta Nielsen, destined to become the first great European star, and directed her in *Life's Tempest* and *A Ballet Dancer's Love*.

A recent restoration of Blom's *Atlantis* shows why Danish films were considered the most sophisticated in the world by 1913. The script, written jointly by Blom and the Nobel laureate Gerhart Hauptmann, is subtle and fast-moving, taking its tormented yet worldly hero from Denmark to Paris, Berlin and New York. The acting is restrained and the portrayal of wealthy middle-class life convincing, while alert to the sexual allure of show-business and a bohemian artist's studio. There is even an alternative Russian tragic ending, specially made for this important export market.

The First World War initially stimulated Danish cinema, making it even more important in Europe, and Blom flourished with such major productions as *The Adventuress*, *The Greatest Love* (1914), *Pro Patria*, *Guilty Love* (1915), and *The World's End* (1916). But after the war, Germany became the new force in Europe and American producers began to dominate the world market. The Danish golden age was over and with it Blom's career.

a film taken long ago: it has not aged, but its spectators have.

Certainly, people were intrigued by the idea that moving images could take on a life of their own, and many early films focused on this fascination. In one ingenious example, *An Animated Picture Studio* (a British film distributed in the US by Biograph, 1903), a young dancer enters a photographic studio and is filmed dancing and then sitting on the photographer's knee. The resulting film is then projected into a picture frame, and when she protests and throws it to the floor, the shattered image continues to move. The dancer in the film is thought to be Isadora Duncan, which makes an already intriguing little allegory even more poignant. Truly—as Wilde might have said—moving pictures could do our living for us.

It was becoming clear they could also have a strange hold over their audiences. Despite being mechanical and photographic, they created a strong psychological relationship. Rudyard Kipling was fascinated by clashes between the primitive and the modern and his 1904 story 'Mrs Bathurst' is probably the first serious attempt to explore the peculiar fascination of the film image. It unfolds as a conversation between sailors, one of whom tells how a ship's stoker takes him to a film show in Cape Town:

'... they had a new turn of a scientific nature called "Home and Friends for a Tickey".'
'Oh, you mean the cinematograph—the pictures of prize-fights and steamers. I've seen 'em up-country.'
'Biograph or cinematograph was what I was alludin' to. London Bridge with the omnibuses—a troopship goin' to the war—marines on parade at Portsmouth, an' the Plymouth Express arrivin' at Paddin'ton.'

The stoker, Vickery, is convinced that a woman he sees in the film of Paddington Station is a Mrs Bathurst that he once knew in Auckland. His companion agrees it looks like her—and has to accompany Vickery every night to see 'perhaps forty-five seconds o' Mrs B. walking down towards us with that blindish look in her eyes', before they get blind drunk together.

During one of these drinking sessions, Vickery reveals his obsession: he believes 'Mrs B.' is looking for *him*, endlessly and vainly. In the end, Vickery is

A 'living picture' in *An Animated Picture Studio* (Biograph, 1903)

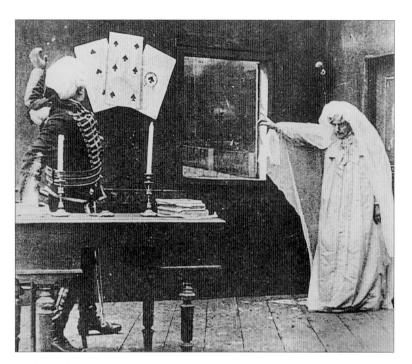

The Queen of Spades (Chardynin, 1910)

found dead up country, the first victim of an obsession with a film—for him the mechanically repeated image of 'Mrs B.' is *more real* than reality itself. Even before there were true fiction films, Kipling understood how it was possible to have an intense fantasy relationship with figures on the screen.

Within ten years, such figures would have their own fantasies, and audiences were being initiated into a much more complex relationship with their unconscious desires and fears. As was suggested in Chapter 2, it had started with dreams. Many early films were presented as dreams made visible, with only a token 'frame' of waking life, or in some cases none at all. But from about 1908, when cinema started to become more self-consciously 'respectable', there was a gradual turn toward realistic story-telling. Now the supernatural and the subjective either lay 'outside' the narrative, or began to be clearly marked off within it as dreams, visions and the like.

This took various forms in different cultures. Often there were widely-held beliefs which both maker and audience shared, making any explicit reference unnecessary. The Biograph films of Griffith, for instance, rest on a set of unspoken religious beliefs which alone explain what are otherwise enigmatic stories. In one of these, two daughters disobey their clergyman father and leave home for a life on the stage. One day we see one of the sisters post a letter on a busy city street. Her father tears it up, unread, but weeps when he is alone. He comes to the theatre where the daughter is also due to give her decision to a suitor. But when she sees her father, she is reconciled with him and abandons the suitor. This, at least, is one interpretation, although others are possible.

The title, of course, tells us it is a morality-play: *At the Crossroads of Life*. It is *about* fateful choices, not mere chance. Behind it stands the biblical injunction to 'honour thy father and mother', and a traditional nonconformist view of the theatre as intrinsically sinful (which seems to have tortured Griffith himself as an actor, and in fact he plays the disappointed suitor in this film). So are we to understand that Divine Providence has brought the father to save his daughter at the crucial moment when she is about to fall irrevocably? It seems we are, which implies that he has somehow been 'led' to respond to the letter we saw posted at the cross-street of a bustling (sinful) city, without having read it. The film seems at pains to stress that this was not a rational response, but one ordained from elsewhere.

Many of Griffith's early films cut between apparently unrelated events, as if to show us that 'something' does connect them. And in a *Biograph Bulletin* announcement for one of these, the rationale is spelled out:

No mortal power can reveal the secrets of the soul. God alone knows our hidden workings even better than we do ourselves.

Griffith has long been credited with developing the technique of 'parallel editing' or cutting to and fro between different strands of action. But what has sometimes been forgotten is that this started as the conscious expression of a severely Christian ideology, in which every action has a moral value and all are eventually held responsible before God for their conduct.

Indeed Griffith appears to have believed that cinema had emerged to fulfil a biblical prophecy. Lillian Gish, who acted in many of his films, recalled him rebuking an actress for using the slang term 'flickers':

He told her never to use that word. She was working in the universal language that had been predicted in the Bible, which was to make all men brothers because they would understand each other. This could end wars and bring about the millennium.

In other cultures, different beliefs were prominent. A number of Russian films around 1910 include ghosts which lure their heroes to a variety of fates. Several of these were adaptations from Russia's national bard, Pushkin, and their use of the supernatural follows a very specific psychological pattern. The river nymphs of Vasili Goncharov's 1910 *Rusalka* lure passers-by to their watery doom, because they are the spirits of maidens who have earlier drowned themselves for betrayed love. Film allowed Goncharov to make the nymph who revenges herself on a faithless prince both ethereal and seductive. Chardynin's 1910 *Queen of Spades* was to be the first of many screen versions of Pushkin's classic ghost story, and it too benefited from being able to show the ghostly Princess as a projection of the hero's guilty conscience.

The supernatural in early Russian cinema is rarely religious in any Christian sense. More commonly it expresses a pagan fatalism, or the visible sign of an inner psychological conflict, as in *The Queen of Spades*. Psychology was indeed what some far-sighted enthusiasts believed cinema would ideally explore. One of these was the popular Russian writer Leonid Andreev, a contemporary and one-time friend of Gorky, who had no doubt that cinema would soon take over many existing functions of theatre. Andreev was already confident in 1911 of:

the revolution in psychology, in the very foundations of thought, that the future Cinema will bring about.

And later in the same 'Letter on Theatre', he continues in similar vein:

If the highest and most sacred aim of art is to instigate contact between people and their own souls, then what an enormous, unimaginable socio-psychological role is destined to be played by this artistic Apache of the present.

At the time Andreev was writing, the best support for his claims would have been the meteoric rise of Danish cinema. From 1910, the output of this small industry created a sensation in many countries—mainly due to its 'sophisticated' treatment of topics that were taboo elsewhere, like seduction, divorce and drugs.

The sophistication consisted mainly of restraint: dealing directly with material that would provoke melodramatic reactions elsewhere. A good example of this cool psychological precision is *Atlantis*, directed by August Blom in 1913 (and newly restored by the Danish Film Archive), which had the distinction of being based on a novel by the winner of the previous year's Nobel Prize for Literature, Gerhart Hauptmann. In almost every respect it was the opposite of the spectacle and sensation films being made elsewhere at the time, and it was widely hailed as a breakthrough—even as an 'improvement' on its source. But there is one striking break in the sober realism of *Atlantis*.

The story is of a man disappointed by the rejection of his scientific work and tormented by his wife's mental illness. He seeks solace in travel and in Berlin meets a dancer, whom he decides to follow to America. The ship, however, hits a wreck and starts to sink. As it does, our hero is dreaming of the legendary sunken city of Atlantis—until panic in the ship's corridors wakens him to the disaster and he joins the lifeboats. The rest of the story need not concern us here, but this single moment of intense subjectivity—a mythic dream that is motivated by a real-life trauma—is a far cry from the simple tit-for-tat dreams of earlier cinema.

It is a dream that belongs fully to the era when the unconscious was first being explored. Although Freud's *Interpretation of Dreams* (1900) had scarcely been a best-seller, the psychoanalytic movement was attracting wide attention in 'advanced' circles. Freud first visited a cinema while in New York in 1909, and was apparently only 'quietly amused'. But he had also published in that year the first of his analytical studies of artists. It dealt with Wilhelm Jensen's story *Gradiva*, about a man who fantasises he is exploring an ancient city. The creators of *Atlantis* must have expected their audience to see a pivotal significance in the scientist's dream which gives the work its title and marks the hero's shift from past to future.

The same year saw, from the underdeveloped German industry, what would be cinema's first demonstration of its ability to conjure a complete, eerily credible world of horror. *The Student of Prague* is set in the same Gothic world as E. T. A. Hoffmann's tales, and it has a similar theme. A poor student sells his reflection to a mysterious stranger in order to court a rich lady, but soon finds that the reflection leads a mocking life of its own. He is drawn into a duel with his beloved's fiancé, whom his double kills. In despair, he finally shoots at the double—and finds he has mortally wounded himself.

Contemporary reviews in Germany were appreciative. Hoffmann's 'Doktor Mirakel' and Wilde's *Dorian Gray* were cited as influences, but none doubted that the film succeeded superbly on its own terms—both as an inspiration for the future:

film is not just a surrogate for this or that art—it is much more a means for creating a self-sufficient and worthy art ...

and as a true horror movie:

The blood races through your veins in a highly satisfactory and ghostly way during this fantastic drama.

The Student of Prague was to have many indirect consequences. Its success encouraged its star, Paul Wegener, to abandon his

stage career with the great Max Reinhardt and throw in his lot with the still dubious cinema. In a 1916 public lecture in Berlin, Wegener proclaimed his faith in a pure cinema that would go beyond both theatre and literature to find its own distinctive poetry. And over the next ten years, he would play a leading part in creating the German Expressionist cinema which triumphantly justified his early confidence.

Virginia Woolf was one of those who responded to the eventual offspring of *The Student of Prague*, the film which made Expressionist cinema widely known: *The Cabinet Doctor of Dr Caligari* (1919). But even while admiring it, she longed for cinema to break free

Baldwin meets his own reflection in *The Student of Prague* (Rye, 1913)

from theatrical representation. A chance obstruction in the projector, which caused a sudden quivering shadow on the screen, was enough to make her wonder:

Is there ... some secret language which we feel and see, but never speak, and, if so, could this be made visible to the eye?

Another fan of *The Student of Prague* was Freud's associate, Otto Rank, who made it the first film to be treated as a psychoanalytic text, when he included it in his study of the 'double'. Stevenson's *Jekyll and Hyde* had given the 'double' a new lease of notoriety as a split personality, but it was to prove an ideal theme for film.

Rank contributed additional chapters to the 1914 edition of *The Interpretation of Dreams* on 'Dreams and Creative Writing' and 'Dreams and Myth'. What he deduced from the survival of the 'double' theme was a constant threat of regression to the primitive, and the continuing presence of primitive fears in modern life—'the return of the repressed'.

And we might speculate that this was what drew the masses to the movies. A chance to return temporarily to primitive emotions and identifications. To lose themselves in the womb-like intimacy of the cinema and forget the demands and discontents of civilisation. To live another life.

The French writer Jules Romains described this collective dream of spectatorship into which the cinema audience passed in a 1911 essay, 'The Crowd at the Cinematograph'. He begins with the idea that entering the darkness of the cinema is like experiencing nightfall or diving underwater:

A bright circle abruptly illuminates the far wall. The whole room seems to sigh, 'Ah!' And through the surprise simulated by this cry, they welcome the resurrection they were certain would come.

The group dream now begins. They sleep; their eyes no longer see. They are no longer conscious of their bodies. Instead there are only passing images, a gliding and rustling of dreams.

Lois Weber

Virtually forgotten until the women's film movement claimed her as a pioneer, Lois Weber (1882–1939) was one of the most famous of all American film-makers in the 'teens. Weber was a teenage piano virtuoso, then a 'home missionary' in the slums of Pittsburgh before going on the stage to earn her living.

Her first film work was as a writer-director and actress for Gaumont Talking Pictures in Cleveland in 1908, while waiting to marry an actor-manager, Phillips Smalley. They joined Reliance, where Griffith would soon work, as an acting duo and writer-directors, before moving in 1912 to Rex, then headed by Porter. Their surviving early films often have striking visual effects—an overhead shot in *Suspense* (1913) and huge close-ups in *Shoes* (1916)—and the Smalleys were soon famous for shock tactics like the female nudity in their crusading *Hypocrites!* (1914).

In 1915, Universal financed Weber's own Hollywood studio, where she and Smalley continued to tackle controversial subjects, like birth control in *Where Are My Children?* and capital punishment in *The People vs John Doe* (both 1916), while maintaining a staunch Christian Science faith. There was also culture: Weber played Portia in *The Merchant of Venice* (1914) and featured the legendary dancer Pavlova in *The Dumb Girl of Portici* (1916).

Independent from 1917, Weber signed a lavish deal with Famous Players in 1920. But her later films failed at the box-office—although it was a restoration of her 1921 drama of middle-class poverty, *The Blot*, that revived her name—and she suffered both a professional and personal collapse in the mid-twenties, before resuming work as a script consultant for Universal in the thirties.

Epilogue *Bringing It All Back Home*

Everywhere in 1913 there were ambitious productions and projects. In France, America and Russia, tough new city films like *Fantômas*, *Traffic in Souls* and *A Child of the Big City* all openly questioned conventional authority and morality, as they displayed their confident new brands of street-level realism. In Germany, *The Student of Prague* reached back into the Romantic period for themes that would inspire a distinctive new national cinema. And in the Scandinavian countries, films like *Atlantis* introduced a fluent psychological realism that was as up-to-date as anything in contemporary literature.

There were many projects, too, for films by established artists in other fields. The Austrian composer Arnold Schoenberg and the Russian abstract painter Wassily Kandinsky were discussing how film might burst the constraints of opera and create a new audiovisual form. Futurists in Russia and Italy took part in several short films celebrating 'Futurist life'. And in France, the Cubist Léopold Survage announced through Apollinaire's new journal his plan to animate a series of rhythmic paintings as 'visual music'.

There is one notable absentee from all these lists. Although the period 1910–13 was one of rapid growth for most national film industries, it was not for Britain. Here producers were slow to accept that audiences wanted longer films and their penny-pinching habits of substituting description for action soon became notorious. A fondness for respectful literary adaptations didn't help, although in more confident hands these might have proved as popular as they did in France and Russia. Meanwhile, the wave of new production from abroad was being eagerly received on British screens.

In 1914, *The Times* reported that only 2 per cent of the million feet of film sold for exhibition in London each week was home-produced. The writing was already on the wall: having been a leading exporter from 1896 to 1907, Britain could now be the first country to have gained and lost a film industry in a little over twenty years. What had gone wrong?

One major problem was clearly that moving pictures had failed to attract lasting support from either business interests or the intelligentsia. In other countries where both these groups became involved at an early stage, the result was dynamic development. In France, for instance, Pathé and Gaumont quickly seized the initiative from Lumière, who remained essentially photographic manufacturers. But as they took the first steps in building their commercial empires, cinema became fashionable in France and attracted the interest of journalists and opinion-formers, as well as leading artists and intellectuals. Soon Pathé and Gaumont saw commercial advantage in allying themselves with these new supporters.

Similar developments took place in Italy, Denmark and Sweden and, belatedly, in Germany. The case of the United States is more complex. Certainly there was early business interest—indeed Edison's attempt to exploit and control 'his' invention consumed much energy which could have gone into production, and the threat of litigation certainly discouraged many, until a licensing trust was

A Study in Scarlet, George Pearson's 1914 Conan Doyle adaptation

established in 1909. It was this very weakness of American production, together with the country's great ethnic diversity, which helped foreign imports gain a foothold in the years before 1913. But once American producers grasped the challenge of longer 'feature' films and West Coast production started— it was in late 1913 that Cecil B. DeMille travelled from New York to a suburb of Los Angeles called Hollywood to make his first film—then American cinema was ready to take on the world. And it did.

There are many Anglo-American ironies in the history of cinema in Britain. Three at least of the early American pioneers were British-born: Edison's original assistant, William Dickson; the cartoonist turned animator J. Stuart Blackton; and the director Herbert Brenon. Blackton and Brenon would eventually return to Britain as major producer-directors, but only near the end of their active careers. But around 1912–13, there was a steady stream of American visitors. The rotund American star, John Bunny, made several comedies for Vitagraph 'on location' in Britain. George Tucker, the director of *Traffic in Souls*, came trailing clouds of notoriety to join the newly established London Film Company. Even Edwin Porter, no longer with Edison, came to Britain briefly in 1914 with plans to produce.

Not all the visitors were American, for cinema was still unfettered by language problems (simply solved by inserting new titles) or prejudices against foreign films. Indeed the first heavily publicised 'exclusive' releases in 1911 were the Italian *Fall of Troy* and a Danish thriller, *In the Hands of Imposters*. Pathé and Gaumont were long established as distributors in

Britain. And in 1913 their French rival, Eclair, came to make a series of Sherlock Holmes films, apparently with the co-operation of Conan Doyle.

Conspicuously missing in Britain, however, were influential figures ready to promote the industrial or cultural status of the new medium, as was already happening elsewhere. British bankers and financiers remained resolutely sceptical, unlike their counterparts abroad. Without such backing, there was little to attract the public figures who could have rallied support for British film-making. Conan Doyle and Rider Haggard, for instance, were among the most popular authors in the world and both interested in cinema, but remained only marginally involved in British film-making. Kipling and Wells had also shown early interest, but played no active role until, in Wells' case, the thirties. In the absence of any lead from such influential prophets of modernity, it is hardly surprising that British cinema continued to seem like a cottage industry until the late twenties, by which time it proved too late to reverse its collapse as an international force.

One of the few established artists who took a practical interest was the narrative painter and Royal Academician Sir Hubert von Herkomer. He established a studio in the grounds of his house at Bushey and with his son plunged into production in 1913. The handful of films he produced before his death a year later were not considered successful (like the vast majority of early British films, they have been lost), but clearly it was early days to judge whether such an intervention might have borne fruit.

Herkomer, not surprisingly, believed that film-making was essentially a visual art:

I see the greatest possibility of art in the film. I do not always find it, certainly, but then I do not always do so throughout an exhibition of paintings or sculpture.

There were a few others who thought like Herkomer. They included the former portrait photographer Elwyn Neame, who joined Hepworth's company; and a one-time *Punch* cartoonist, Harry Furniss, who had worked for Edison in the United States, before returning to Britain and going into production on his own account in 1914. Furniss, too, thought visual training was valuable:

As an artist who, all his life, has posed models and arranged pictures ... I have been a director of composition—of movement.

The idea of film as a visual art might seem uncontroversial, even obvious. But it seems to have struck relatively few in Britain during the early years. Perhaps this was indicative of a wider prejudice in British culture. John Carey's provocative study of British intellectuals' hostility to the masses quotes a reaction to the appearance of the *Daily Mirror* as an illustrated newspaper in 1903:

women habitually think in pictures ... when men think pictorially, they unsex themselves.

Pictorial thinking, of course, needed to develop into filmic thinking. One untypical British venture from 1916, which was coincidentally shot at Herkomer's former studio, offers a tantalising glimpse of what *might* have been possible if there had not been such a gulf between the wider arts community and what was already known as 'the film trade'. It started with an actor who had taken over Herkomer's studio asking the famous playwright James Barrie for a film script. Barrie responded instantly with *The Real Thing At Last*, a burlesque on *Macbeth* which he intriguingly subtitled 'A suggestion for Artists of the Future'. The basic idea was a humorous contrast between a polite British production of 'the Scottish murder mystery' and a vigorous American one.

According to the memoirs of those who took part, the atmosphere was informal and enthusiastic, with Barrie himself undertaking most of the direction. The actors were of high calibre and expected to show the same commitment as Barrie while he improvised at high speed:

Barrie thought Leslie Henson's profile was like Shakespeare's, so he added a frame story in which Henson, photographed in Shakespeare's house in Stratford, appeared as the dramatist, pacing up and down his bedroom and waiting for a telephone call from New York. In the finished picture, the conversation appeared in subtitles:

'Yes! Shakespeare speaking. How did they like *Macbeth* in New York?'

'*Macbeth* is sure-fire! What price your next play?'

William 'Buffalo Bill' Cody re-enacting an 1876 exploit from his own legendary career in a 1913 film

Other details remembered include a telegram delivered on horseback which read: 'If Birnam Wood moves, it's a cinch'. The British witches apparently stirred a very small cauldron, while an American chorus of 'cuties' danced round their large one. Similarly, the climactic duel was shown both in a muddy ditch and on top of a skyscraper. The British version ended with genteel understatement: 'The elegant home of the Macbeths is no longer a happy one'; while the American version concluded more optimistically: 'The Macbeths repent and all ends happily.'

The film received its premiere at a special Royal Command war charity performance in 1916, with an elaborate staging. All the cast were present and went up on stage, only to disappear through a door before they magically reappeared in the film, which had a running commentary by Edward Gwenn and music by the composer of *Chu Chin Chow*. Although the presentation and subsequent release was considered a great success by the film's makers, it provoked a stern rebuke from one of the film trade papers, which described it as unsuitable entertainment for royalty in wartime and an unfair lampoon of both the film industry and American attitudes to Shakespeare!

No copy of *The Real Thing At Last* is known to exist, so we may never be able to judge whether it was more than a light-hearted romp. But all the evidence suggests that Barrie was excited by the invitation to make a film and took it seriously—which of course did not mean solemnly. Amid the prevailing dull climate of British production, it suggests a wit and intelligence which also seems to have struck a popular chord. For the problem which British film-makers proved even less able to solve than their contemporaries in other media was how to create a new popular culture that was not merely nostalgic or derivative.

Meanwhile, that problem was being solved elsewhere. While other European film-makers were experimenting desperately to compete with the strength and volume of American exports, one particular American genre had already captured the mass audience and given cinema a common international currency. A song from a British revue of the period neatly summed it up:

The films which people like the best are of the cowboy kind
The plots are nearly all the same, but no one seems to mind.

'The Cinema Operator' (1914)

Everywhere audiences flocked to see Westerns, whatever other films they might also watch. They were as popular across Europe and throughout its far-flung empires as in the United States itself. How had this come about and what did it mean?

The appeal of the American West was already wide and deep before moving pictures. Queen Victoria was only one of countless unlikely Western fans, and her introduction had been through Buffalo Bill's Wild West. The story goes that she broke her twenty-five-year mourning for the death of Prince Albert to see the show a second time, after being so stirred by its daredevil displays and dramatic re-enactments at a private performance in 1887. A month later, at

Broncho Billy Anderson (at right) in *Bronco Billy's Adventure*

another London performance, four European kings occupied the Deadwood Stage, with Prince Edward riding beside Buffalo Bill as he drove.

It is an astonishing image for us today. If Buffalo Bill could lift the spirits of the notoriously unamused Queen and attract Europe's monarchs to his frontier mythology, what could he not do? One recent writer, Jane Tompkins, suggests we might even see him as a 'secular messiah', someone semi-divine whom millions believed could rescue them from the routine and the banal by his marvellous presence.

There was at least no denying William 'Buffalo Bill' Cody's immense popularity and the lasting legacy he left as our image of the legendary West. Indeed, history, fiction and legend were thoroughly confused from the outset. For there were dime novels about 'Buffalo Bill' while Cody was still a part-time Army scout in the Indian wars and was starting to appear as an entertainer on stage. And this fertile confusion, further enhanced by the photographic realism of film, was an important part of the Western's appeal.

The icons of the 'true' American West who were filmed for the Kinetoscope in New Jersey in 1895—Sioux Indians performing traditional dances and Annie Oakley demonstrating her celebrated shooting skills—were already stars of Buffalo Bill's Wild West (apparently he never used the word 'show', presumably to preserve the illusion of authenticity).

History was not what attracted Cody's audiences, or the readers of Western dime novels, or the viewers of *Kit Carson* and *The Pioneers*—two of the first film Westerns, directed by Wallace McCutcheon

in the Adirondacks in 1903. But it was an important part of the legend and authenticity, of a kind, mattered greatly. Westerns had to keep faith with the mythic Frontier and respect their audience's expectations. In return, audiences showed devout loyalty.

The first star of screen Westerns was Gilbert Anderson. Between 1907 and 1914, this former travelling salesman and jobbing actor appeared in some 400 short films as 'Broncho Billy'. The continuing success of these made him one of the first established 'characters' in cinema—a contemporary of Linder's 'Max', but with wider appeal—and the prototype of all future cowboy heroes.

The Broncho Billy films were simple and direct, but also varied and dramatically efficient. *Broncho Billy and the Sheriff's Kid* (1913), for instance, starts with Billy breaking out of jail by holding up the sheriff, only to come across the sheriff's baby girl fallen over a cliff. He hesitates, but decides to take her home and run the risk of being recaptured. *Broncho Billy's Buried Letters* (1910) strikes a tragic note. Billy is first seen getting hastily married before setting off with his best friend to prospect for gold. He doesn't realise that his friend is jealous and is intercepting letters from Billy's wife to sour their relationship. Only when the pair are surrounded by Indians and the friend is mortally wounded, does he reveal the cache of hidden letters.

It is still easy to understand, and feel, the universal appeal of these simple moralities. But it would be wrong to assume that Westerns, even at this early stage, were essentially artless. For Anderson and his successor William S. Hart inherited not only the dime novel legacy, but also a vigorous stage tradition. Hart had been a noted Shakespearean actor on Broadway before he became even more famous in a spectacular 1899 *Ben-Hur* and in the stage versions of such Western classics as *The Squaw Man* and *The Virginian*. The DeMille brothers, William and his younger brother Cecil, grew up in the New York theatre world which was dominated by the producer David Belasco. It was Belasco who married melodrama and realism; and one of his popular plays provided the libretto for Puccini's 1910 'Western' opera *The Girl of the Golden West.*

So when Cecil DeMille travelled west in 1913 to film *The Squaw Man*, he was certainly no unsophisticated innocent. Two years earlier, his brother had given a lecture at Columbia University on 'Dramatic Technique and Modern Ideals' which could stand as a manifesto for what they and many of the founders of Hollywood believed:

unlike good literature, good drama is a relative term depending on certain limitations as to time, place and the nature of the audience for which it is written ... A play achieves it purpose, and its only dramaturgic purpose, when it holds and moves its audience.

Westerns knew their audience. They appeared, not in the guise of art, but of a compelling entertainment which cut across boundaries of nationality, class and education. Set in a mythic landscape and dealing in moral certainties, they also had a progressive, democratic appeal—and not only to men, as an American popular song of 1912 shows:

**Oh! Lovie Joe, want to go to a picture show, let's go to-night,
One 'bout the west, it's the best, nothing like the rest, Gee! it's some sight,
Where maidens fair do and dare in the prairie air ...**

'Moving Picture Rag'

Their success carried a lesson for producers and artists everywhere. Put bluntly, it was that this upstart popular art had created its own audience and set its own standards. The new ground rules were

The Girl of the Golden West (DeMille, 1915): the film of the play of the opera

summarised by a leading exponent of the history of fine art, Erwin Panofsky, who also appreciated the newest entry to the pantheon:

The movies have reestablished that dynamic contact between art production and art consumption which ... is sorely attentuated, if not entirely interrupted, in many other fields of artistic endeavor. Whether we like it or not, it is the movies that mold, more than any other single force, the opinions, the taste, the language, the dress, the behavior, and even the physical appearance of a public comprising more than 60 per cent of the population of the earth.

In doing so they had served notice on traditional 'high' art, which would henceforth have to justify itself in the era of the movies.

If all the serious lyric poets, composers, painters and sculptors were forced by law to stop their activities, a rather small fraction of the general public would become aware of the fact and a still smaller fraction would seriously regret it. If the same thing were to happen with the movies the social consequences would be catastrophic.

Panofsky was born in 1892 and had grown up with the movies. He had no doubt that they were as much art as anything else being produced with that aspiration in the twentieth century and he described them, provocatively, as the modern equivalent of the great medieval cathedrals.

Meanwhile, in the Moorish and Art Deco splendour of the picture palaces, his whole generation was growing up with the movies and imbibing their powerful new language of fantasy. Among those anonymous spectators were the future Hitler, Stalin, Mussolini and Franco, each of whom developed an intense relationship with the screen. They would make use of cinema to impose their vision of a 'new life', creating studios, dictating subjects and scenarios, censoring and fantasising. Life under their regimes would become, vaingloriously and grimly, like being trapped in a movie.

To be fair, a passion for cinema was not exclusive to dictators. Churchill and Franklin Roosevelt were as much in thrall to movies as their opponents in the Second World War. So too were Einstein, Picasso, Jung, Wittgenstein and countless other leading figures of the last hundred years, together with the anonymous masses who were their neighbours before the screen.

For it was in the darkness of the cinema that the century found its escape from an increasingly confused and congested reality, and its only certainties. The movies became its collective unconscious— the fantasy life of the twentieth century.

Notes and Sources

Notes

Works referred to more than once are listed alphabetically at the end of the Notes and indicated here only by author and date.

Introduction

Hollis Frampton's 'For a Metahistory of Film', originally published in *Artforum*, September 1971, is reprinted in Frampton's *Circles of Confusion* (1983). His films are distributed by the London Filmmakers Co-op. For new approaches to early film history, see: Burch (1990), Elsaesser and Barker (1990), Hansen (1991), Musser (1991). Edward FitzGerald's translation of the 12th-century Persian poet, *The Rubáiyát of Omar Khayyám*, was first published in 1859. W. K. L. Dickson and Antonia Dickson's *History of the Kinetograph, Kinetoscope and Kinetophonograph* appeared in 1895. The Li Hung Chang film, like most other early American titles mentioned here, is preserved in the Library of Congress Paper Print Collection, Washington, DC, which is catalogued in Niver (1985). On the Moscow Art Theatre's 'cinematograph' style, see Yuri Tsivian, 'Early Russian cinema: some observations', in Taylor and Christie (1991), p. 26. Debussy's two books of *Preludes* (1909–13) are vividly contrasted short pieces with unusual titles, suggesting a mixed early film programme; and of Thomas Hardy's massive 'epic-drama' *The Dynasts* (1904–8), the *Oxford Companion to English Literature* remarks: 'the cinematic nature of the work has often been noted'. The Pittsburgh eye-witness account is by Elizabeth Butler, in *Women and the Trades: Pittsburgh, 1907–8* (New York, 1909), quoted by Garth S. Jowett, 'The First Motion Picture Audiences', in Fell (1983). Tarkovsky's ideas on time appear in ch. 3 of his *Sculpting in Time* (London, 1986). 'The Cinematograph Train' by G. E. Farrow is quoted in Chanan (1980).

1 Space and Time Machine

The London Lumière show report in *The Sketch*, 18 March 1896, is quoted in Tsivian (1994). Gorky's article is translated in Taylor and Christie (1988), p. 25. Kipling's story 'Mrs Bathurst' appeared in his 1904 collection *Traffics and Discoveries*. The Arrival of a Train/Anna Karenina association is documented in Tsivian (1994), pp. 137–44. Quotations from Hugo, Ruskin, Flaubert and Heine appear in Wolfgang Schivelbusch, *The Railway Journey* (New York, 1979). The opening of ch. 3 of *Through the Looking-Glass* (1872) is set in a railway carriage. Dickens' rail crash experience is described in Claire Tomalin, *The Invisible Woman* (London, 1990). *The Wind in the Willows* was first published in 1908. Futurist Manifesto quotation from Umbro Apollonio (ed.), *Futurist Manifestos* (London, 1973), p. 21. Octave Mirbeau, 'La 628-E8' (1908), quoted in Stephen Kern, *The Culture of Time and Space 1880–1918* (London, 1983), p. 113. Bely's essay 'The City' is quoted in Tsivian (1994), pp. 150–1. Verne's *20,000 Leagues Under the Sea* appeared in 1869 and his *Around the World in Eighty Days*, of which Phileas Fogg is the hero, in 1873. Oliver Wendell Holmes' 'Doings of the Sunbeam' first appeared in the *Atlantic Monthly* (1863) and is reprinted in Beaumont Newhall (ed.) *Photography: Essays and Images* (New York, 1980), pp. 63–77. H. G. Wells' *The Time Machine* had started as a series of magazine articles in 1888, before being rewritten as a novel. Two of Henri Bergson's books were widely influential: *Matter and Memory* (1896) and *Creative Evolution* (1907). Marcel Proust's novel series, 1913–27, was originally translated by C. K. Scott-Moncrieff as *Remembrance of Things Past*. Paul's patent application is quoted in Ramsaye (1926), pp. 155–7. An International Conference on Time held in Paris in 1912 led to international standardisation. Frederick Taylor proposed the 'scientific management' of work in 1883. The editorial is from the *St Louis Post Despatch* and is quoted without date in Ramsaye, pp. 159–60. Parallels between Méliès and Freud are explored by Anne-Marie Quévrain and Marie-George Charconnet-Méliès, 'Méliès et Freud', in Madeleine Malthête-Méliès (ed.), *Méliès et la naissance du spectacle cinématographique* (Paris, 1984).

2 Tales from the City

The traditional view of the Bazar de la Charité fire is given by Ramsaye (1926), pp. 353–7; the Montesquiou duel is described in Roger Shattuck,

The Banquet Years (New York, 1971), p. 13; and evidence against the traditional account is cited in Crafton (1990), pp. 98, 320. 'The Machine Stops' was first published in 1909 and is now included in Forster's *Collected Short Stories* (London, 1947). The Goncourts' journal is quoted in T. J. Clark, *The Painting of Modern Life* (Princeton, 1984), p. 34. Charles Baudelaire, 'The Painter of Modern Life' (1863); this translation from G. Bruno, *Streetwalking on a Ruined Map* (Princeton, 1993), pp. 48–9. Blok's letter quoted in Tsivian (1994), p. 40. Thomas Carlyle, *Sartor Resartus* (first pub. 1833; London, 1896), p. 16. Emile Durkheim's study of crime was published in 1893, and his *Suicide* in 1897; Simon LeBon's *The Crowd: A Study of the Popular Mind* in 1895, and Georg Simmel's 'The Metropolis and Mental Life' in 1900. On the background to and making of *Life of an American Fireman*, see Musser (1991), pp. 212–34. On Andrei Bely and *That Fatal Sneeze*, see Tsivian (1994), pp. 151–3. Bely's *Petersburg* was first published in 1916. On Joyce's 1909 cinema venture, see Richard Ellmann, *James Joyce* (Oxford, 1966), p. 310ff; Liam O'Leary, *Cinema Ireland 1896–1950* (Dublin, 1990); and Brenda Maddox, *Nora: A Biography of Nora Joyce* (London, 1988), p. 135ff. Samuel Beckett's letter to Eisenstein is reproduced in J. Leyda (ed.), *Eisenstein 2: A Premature Celebration of Eisenstein's Centenary* (Calcutta, 1985; London, 1988), p. 59. Apollinaire's 'Un beau film' first appeared in 1907; a translation, 'A Great Film', appears in R. Shattuck (ed.), *Apollinaire: Selected Writings* (New York, 1971), pp. 238–41. See also P. Hammond, 'Kostrowitzky's Kinema', *Afterimage* (UK) 10, Autumn 1981, pp. 56–69. On kinetoscope parlours and nickelodeons, see David Q. Bowers, *Nickelodeon Theatres and Their Music* (New York, 1986); British exhibition and 'penny gaffs' are covered in Low II, p. 14ff; the Odessa account is in Tsivian (1994), p. 16. The American review of *Nero* is from *Moving Picture World*. On the naming of cinemas, see Bowers (1986), and F. Lacloche, *Architectures de cinémas* (Paris, 1981). The St Petersburg cinemas of Vasilyeva are described in Tsivian (1994), p. 24. Biograph's publicity for *The Musketeers of Pig Alley* is quoted in Brownlow (1990), p. 184. Baudelaire translated Poe's 'The Murder of Marie Roget' in 1848; the first Sherlock Holmes story appeared in 1887. Marcel Allain and Pierre Souvestre produced 32 Fantômas novels between 1911–13; Feuillade's serial was based on the first five. Tsivian discusses 'Russian endings' in Taylor and Christie (1991), pp. 7–8.

3 The Body Electric
The Annabelle Moore affair is recounted by Ramsaye (1926), pp. 333–40. *Frankenstein* was published in 1818. This extract from *The Future Eve* appears in Annette Michelson, 'On the Eve of the Future', *October*, 29, 1984, pp. 2–21. Edison's hope of linking recorded sound and vision comes in his preface to the Dicksons' 1895 booklet, *History of the Kinetograph*. Muybridge's killing of his wife's lover is narrated in Ramsaye (1926), pp. 21–49. The *Alta California* newspaper article of 1880 is quoted in Coe (1992), p. 18. For Frampton's view of Muybridge, see 'Eadweard Muybridge: Fragments of a Tesseract', in Frampton (1983), p. 79. Background to Edison's 'Sneeze' is from Williams (1990), pp. 51–2. On early voyeur and 'keyhole' films, see André Gaudreault (ed.), *Ce que je vois de mon ciné …* (Paris, 1988), and Burch (1990), pp. 222–4. The letter from Butte is quoted in Ramsaye (1926), p. 256. On postcards, see P. Hammond, *French Undressing* (London, 1976). I am grateful to Luke McKernan for bringing the Bamforth catalogue entry for *Women's Rights* to my attention. The Bioscope review of *Fifty Years of Paris Fashions* is quoted in Elizabeth Leese, *Costume Design in the Movies* (New York/London, 1991), p. 9. Duchamp's account of his 'Nude Descending a Staircase' is from Pierre Cabanne, *Entretiens avec Marcel Duchamp* (Paris, 1967), p. 49. On Cohl and early animation, see Crafton (1990). Siegfried Sassoon's poem appears in Philip French and Ken Wlaschin, *The Faber Book of Movie Verse* (London, 1993), p. 38.

4 Real Lives
Paul's Derby presentation is described in Barnes (1976), p. 112. The McKinley assassination sequence of films are held by the Library of Congress and have also been transferred to video disc. On the Magic Lantern, see Coe (1981), ch. 1. On travel lecturers, see Theodore X. Barber, 'The Roots of Travel Cinema', *Film History* 5.1, March 1993.

Dostoevsky visited the Crystal Palace in 1862. On Barnum, see Neil Hamilton, *Humbug: The Art of P. T. Barnum* (Chicago and London, 1981). Emmanuelle Toulet, 'Cinema at the Universal Exposition, Paris, 1900' is translated in *Persistence of Vision*, 9, 1991, pp. 10–36. The Cinéorama, the Lumière giant projection and early sound at the exposition are all documented in Toulet (1988), pp. 42–3, 47–8 and 104–6. Doublier is quoted in Stephen Bottomore, 'Dreyfus and Documentary', *Sight & Sound*, Autumn 1984, p. 290. Williamson's catalogue entry for *A Big Swallow* appears in Low I, p. 75. Doyen's difficulties are discussed in Toulet (1990), pp. 74–5, and in *Le cinéma des origines* (Paris, 1976), pp. 101–5. On Starewicz, see Jayne Pilling (ed.), *Starewicz 1882–1965* (Edinburgh, 1983). The Secretary of the National Education Association and Sir Ray Lankester are both quoted in Low II, pp. 40 and 38 respectively. Bergson is quoted in Crafton (1990), p. 325. Herbert Ponting's own written account of the expedition was titled *The Great White South* (London, 1921); see also H. J. P. Arnold, *Photographer of the World* (London, 1969). Virginia Woolf's essay 'The Cinema' was first published in *The New Republic* (1926), pp. 308–11. Pirandello's original title was *Shooting (Si gira!)*, but he changed it in 1925 to *The Notebooks of Serafino Gubbio, Cameraman*.

5 *The Waking Dream*

The two Paris newspapers which reviewed the Lumière demonstration of 28 December on the 30th were *La Poste* and *Le Radicale*; their articles are quoted in Toulet (1988), pp. 134–5. Sir David Brewster's account of the Phantasmagoria in his *Letters on Natural Magic* (1834) is quoted in Coe (1981), p. 14. Pauline Chapman, *Madame Tussaud in England* (London, 1992) gives a useful history of the wax museum and quotes Cruikshank's verse (p. 79). Eisenstein's memories of the Musée Grévin are in the chapter called 'Souvenirs d'enfance' in Richard Taylor (ed.), *Beyond the Stars: the Memoirs of Sergei Eisenstein* (London and Calcutta, 1995). Details of the Clark 'waxworks' Kinetoscope productions are in Musser (1991), p. 56. On X-rays, see Yuri Tsivian, 'X-rays, the Microscope and the Notion of "Penetrating Vision" in Avant-garde and Pre-Narrative Film Culture' which cites Otto Glasser's account of the 1896 Edison New York show. Smith's catalogue description of *Photographing a Ghost* is in Low I, pp. 78–9. Details of the magicians who influenced Méliès and quotation from his memoirs in David Robinson, *Georges Méliès: Father of Film Fantasy* (London, 1993). On F. Holland Day's religious photography, see C. Keil, '*From the Manger to the Cross*: The New Testament Narrative and the Question of Stylistic Retardation', in Cosandey (1992), p. 114. The fullest account of early American Passion films is C. Musser, 'Les Passions et les Mystères de la Passion aux Etats-Unis (1880–1900)', in Cosandey (1992), pp. 146–86; see also Ramsaye (1926), pp. 366–78. Col. Hadley's prediction is recorded in Ramsaye (1926), p. 375. The Joye Collection is outlined by R. Cosandey, 'L'abbé Joye, une collection, une pratique: Première approche', in Cosandey (1992), pp. 60–70. On Jewish reactions to *The Life of Moses*, see Hansen (1991), p. 113. On Tissot and *From the Manger to the Cross*, see Herbert Reynolds, 'From the Palette to the Screen', in Cosandey (1992), pp. 275–310. On The Photo-Drama of Creation, see R. A. Nelson, 'Propaganda for God' in Cosandey (1992), pp. 230–55. The *New York Times* review of *Quo Vadis?* is quoted in Richard Schickel, *D. W. Griffith: an American Life* (New York, 1984), p. 188. Moréas' 'Manifesto of Symbolism' appeared in *Le Figaro littéraire*, 18 September 1886. Gorky's article is translated in Taylor and Christie (1988), p. 25. The *Biograph Bulletin* is quoted in Adam Knee, 'The Spirituality of D. W. Griffith's Editing', in Cosandey (1992), p. 326. Lillian Gish's recollection of Griffith is quoted in Hansen (1991), p. 77. Andreev's 'Letter on Cinema' is translated in Taylor and Christie (1988), pp. 27–31. *Atlantis*, newly restored by the Danish Film Archive, was shown at the Pordenone Silent Film Festival, Le Giornate del Cinema Muto, in 1993, as was *The Student of Prague*, also in a restoration. Wegener's speech is quoted in Kristin Thompson, 'Some Links Between German Fantasy Films of the Teens and Twenties', in Paolo Cherchi Usai and Lorenzo Codelli (eds.), *Before Caligari: German Cinema 1895–1920* (Pordenone, 1990), pp. 142–4. Otto Rank's essay on 'The Double' is summarised in S. S. Prawer, *Caligari's Children: The Film as Tale of Terror* (Oxford, 1980), pp. 118–20.

Jules Romains' 'The Crowd at the Cinematograph' is translated in Richard Abel, *French Film Theory and Criticism, 1907–39* (Princeton, 1983) vol. 1, p. 53.

Epilogue

Details of Schoenberg's, Kandinsky's, Piccasso's and Survage's film projects appear in Standish Lawder, *The Cubist Cinema* (New York, 1975). Herkomer and Furniss are quoted in Low II, pp. 262, 263. Holbrook Jackson on 'unmanly' visual thinking is quoted in John Carey, *The Intellectuals and the Masses* (London, 1992), p. 8. Barrie's *The Real Thing At Last* is noted in Luke McKernan and Olwen Terris, *Walking Shadows: Shakespeare in the National Film and Television Archive* (London, 1994), p. 6; fuller details are given in Robert H. Ball, *Shakespeare on Silent Film: A Strange Eventful History* (London, 1968), pp. 222–6. The songs are quoted in Theodore van Houten, *Silent Cinema Music* (Buren, The Netherlands, 1992). I am grateful to Ed Buscombe for information about Buffalo Bill's Wild West, and to his *Companion to the Western* (London, 1993) for further background and detail on Westerns. Jane Tompkins' account of Buffalo Bill is in *West of Everything* (New York and Oxford, 1992), pp. 195–203. William DeMille was talking to New York students in 1911, quoted in Paolo Cherchi Usai and Lorenzo Codelli (eds.), *The DeMille Legacy* (Pordenone, 1991), p.106. Erwin Panofsky's essay, 'Style and Medium in the Motion Pictures', was originally given as a talk at Princeton to promote a proposed film department at the Museum of Modern Art in New York, and published in 1934, then revised in 1947. Quotations here are from Daniel Talbot (ed.), *Film: An Anthology* (Berkeley, 1966), pp. 16–17.

Sources

John Barnes, *The Beginnings of the Cinema in England* (London, 1976)
_____, *Filming the Boer War* (London, 1992)
Kevin Brownlow, *Behind the Mask of Innocence: Films of Social Conscience in the Silent Era* (London, 1990)
Noël Burch, *Life to Those Shadows* (London, 1990)

Michael Chanan, *The Dream That Kicks* (London, 1980)
Brian Coe, *A History of Movie Photography* (London, 1981)
_____, *Muybridge and the Chronophotographers* (London, 1992)
Roland Cosandey, André Gaudreault, Tom Gunning (eds.), *An Invention of the Devil? Religion and Early Cinema* (Montreal and Lausanne, 1992), referred to as 'Cosandey (1992)'
Donald Crafton, *Emile Cohl, Caricature, and Film* (Princeton, 1990)
Thomas Elsaesser and Adam Barker (eds.), *Early Cinema: Space, Frame, Narrative* (London, 1990)
John L. Fell (ed.), *Film Before Griffith* (Berkeley, 1983)
Hollis Frampton, *Circles of Confusion* (Rochester, 1983)
Miriam Hansen, *Babel and Babylon: Spectatorship in American Silent Film* (Cambridge, MA/London, 1991)
Rachael Low and Roger Manvell, *The History of the British Film, 1896–1906* (London, 1948), referred to as 'Low I'
Rachael Low, *The History of the British Film, 1906–1914* (London, 1948), 'Low II'
Charles Musser, *Before the Nickelodeon: Edwin S. Porter and the Edison Manufacturing Company* (Berkeley, 1991)
Kemp R. Niver, *Early Motion Pictures* (Washington, 1985)
Terry Ramsaye, *A Million and One Nights: A History of the Motion Picture Through 1925* (New York, 1926; 1986 facsimile ed.)
Richard Taylor and Ian Christie (eds.), *The Film Factory: Russian and Soviet Cinema in Documents, 1896–1939* (London, 1988)
_____, *Inside the Film Factory* (London, 1991)
Emmanuelle Toulet, *Cinématographe, invention du siècle* (Paris, 1988)
Yuri Tsivian, *Early Cinema in Russia and Its Cultural Reception* (London, 1994)
Linda Williams, *Hard Core: Power, Pleasure and the 'Frenzy of the Visible'* (London, 1990)

Finding Out More

If you want to find out more about early cinema at first hand, the following is a brief guide to UK organisations with relevant collections, publications and interests. Those in **A** *are open to the public, while an appointment will usually be necessary for organisations listed in* **B** *.*

A   Public Museums and Collections

The Museum of the Moving Image
MOMI is an award-winning museum with a difference. Its unique collection of equipment and memorabilia spans the whole history of 'moving images' from shadow-puppets to the latest electronic techniques, with a cast of actor-guides to help bring the history alive. 'Countdown to Cinema' is a programme of special events running through the Centenary period, with lectures, demonstrations and workshops.
Open 10.00–6.00 daily, including Bank Holidays (closed Christmas Eve, Christmas Day and Boxing Day). South Bank, Waterloo, London SE1 8XT. 0171–401 2636

National Museum of Photography, Film and Television
A branch of the Science Museum devoted to the art and science of photography, film and television, exploring the relationship of equipment, chemistry and electronics to the images they produce. With many 'hands-on' displays, a Cinerama theatre and Britain's only IMAX cinema.
Open Tues–Sun, 10.30–6.00. Pictureville, Bradford, West Yorks BD1 1NQ. 01274–727488

Science Museum
Collection of pre-cinema and early cinema equipment.
Open Mon–Sat 10.00–6.00, Sun 11.00–6.00. Exhibition Road, London SW7 2DD. 0171–938 8000

Hove Museum and Art Gallery
Hove and Brighton pioneers' collection, including many of the films viewable on video.

Open Tues–Fri 10.00–5.00, Sat 10.00–4.30, Sun 2.00–5.00. 19 New Church Road, Hove, East Sussex BN3 4AB. 01273–779410

Kingston Museum
The Eadweard Muybridge photographic collection.
Open Mon, Tues, Thur–Sat, 10.00–5.00. Wheatfield Way, Kingston upon Thames KT1 2PS.
0181–546 5386

B   Archives

British Film Institute
The National Film and Television Archive holds approximately 200,000 titles covering the whole span of moving-image history. The Cataloguing Section compiles detailed information about the collection, and the Viewing Service provides access for bona fide researchers and students. Stills Posters and Designs holds some six million images from 60,000 titles, together with posters, and set and costume designs. 21 Stephen Street, London W1P 2LN. 0171–255 1444

Imperial War Museum
The IWM Department of Film preserves and makes accessible a wide range of war-related film, dating from 1902. Regular public screenings and individual and group viewings for research purposes are provided. Some material is available for loan to higher educational institutions, and a series of video cassettes may be purchased for private use. Lambeth Road, London SE1 6HZ. 0171–416 5291

East Anglian Film Archive
Documentary films of the Eastern region from 1902 to the present. Mon–Fri 9.00–5.00. Centre for East Anglian Studies, University of East Anglia, Norwich NR4 7TJ. 01603–592664

Scottish Film Archive
Holds a non-fiction collection of material from 1896 to the present. Mon–Fri, 9.30–5.00. Dowanhill, 74 Victoria Crescent Road, Glasgow G12 9JN.
0141–334 4445

Wales Film and Television Archive

A mixed collection dating from 1911 to the present. WFTVA, Unit 1, Aberystwyth Science Park, Cefn Llan, Aberystwyth, Dyfed SY23 3AH. 01970–626007

Wessex Film and Sound Archive

Non-fiction collection from 1900 to present. Mon–Fri, 9.00–5.00. Hampshire Record Office, Sussex Street, Winchester SO23 8TH. 01962–847742

C Organisations and Societies

Cinema 100

The organisation established to promote a nationwide celebration of 100 years of cinema in the UK during 1996. With members from all branches of the cinema and film industries, its aim is to ensure these celebrations reach and involve the widest possible audience. For details of events and activity taking place throughout the UK, contact Cinema 100 at 10 Stephen Mews, London W1P 0AX. 0171–636 7214

Cinema Theatres Association

The CTA promotes interest in all aspects of cinema buildings, and campaigns for their preservation and continued use. It maintains an archive, arranges visits and lectures, and publishes the bi-monthly *CTA Bulletin*, a members' newsletter. Inquiries to: The Membership Secretary, Flat 30, Cambridge Court, Cambridge Road, Southend-on-Sea, Essex SS1 1EJ.

Domitor

The international association to promote the study of early cinema publishes a regular Bulletin and holds a bi-annual conference on a major theme within early cinema. Membership: c/o Carlos Bustamante, Filminstitut HdK, Hochschule der Künste Berlin, Postfach 12 67 20, D-1000 Berlin 12.

Magic Lantern Society

Founded 1975. Aims to revive and sustain the art of magic lantern projection, with an interest in all aspects of pre-cinema, including shadow-shows, dioramas, optical toys, peep-shows and the beginnings of film. Publishes the *New Magic Lantern*

Journal, *MLS Newsletter*, books and reprints. Inquiries to: The Secretary, 'Prospect', High Street, Nutley, East Sussex TN22 3NH.

Projected Picture Trust

Founded in 1979 to preserve and conserve cinema equipment, the Trust publishes a quarterly magazine and is active in six UK regions with a variety of conservation and demonstration projects. Inquiries to: PPT, Ernest Lindgren House, Kingshill Way, Berkhamsted HP4 3TP.

D Films to Rent and Buy

BFI Distribution has a wide selection of early films available on 35mm and 16mm for rental. Details of these are in a special *Early and Silent Film* catalogue, available from BFI Distribution, 21 Stephen Street, London W1P 2LN. 0171–255 1444

Also available for purchase from BFI Distribution are a number of video compilations, including *Early Cinema* vols 1 and 2, a ten-volume set *Early Russian Cinema* (also available singly) and a selection from the first British newsreel, *Topical Budget*.

Connoisseur and Academy Video are specialist video labels, published by the BFI. Their catalogues includes a growing number of early cinema titles, including Griffith's *Birth of a Nation*, Ponting's *90° South* and documentaries on Chaplin, Keaton, Lloyd and Griffith by Kevin Brownlow and David Gill. Releases in 1995 include Werner Nekes' *Film Before Film* and Anthony Slide's *America's Silent Feminists*. Connoisseur and Academy releases are available from all good video suppliers, or by mail order from Connoisseur Video, 10a Stephen Mews, London W1P 0AX.

Index